OPEN WORLD

T0349657

A2

KEY

**WORKBOOK
WITH ANSWERS**

with Audio Download

Frances Treloar

Cambridge University Press
www.cambridge.org/elt

Cambridge Assessment English
www.cambridgeenglish.org

Information on this title: www.cambridge.org/9781108753272

© Cambridge University Press and UCLES 2019

First published 2019

20 19 18 17 16 15 14 13 12 11 10 9 8 7 6 5

Printed in Great Britain by CPI Group (UK) Ltd, Croydon CR0 4YY

A catalogue record for this publication is available from the British Library

isbn 978-1-108-75327-2 Workbook with answers with Audio Download

CONTENTS

S WHO I AM

VOCABULARY

1 Complete the table with family words. Some words are the same for men and women.

WOMAN/GIRL	MAN/BOY
grandmother	**1** ....
2	nephew
wife	**3** ....
4	son
aunt	**5** ....
6	cousin
child	**7** ....
8	brother
grandparent	**9** ....
10	grandpa/granddad
mum/mother	**11** ....
12	grandson

2 Complete the sentences with a country or a nationality.

1 Peter is .... He's from Detroit in the USA.
2 Luis is Mexican. He's from the south of ....
3 João's from Lisbon in Portugal, so he's ....
4 Nick's mum is from Canada and his dad is from ...., so he's half .... and half French!
5 Jiao is from Hainan in .... so she's Chinese.
6 Luca's family are from Milan in Italy, so he's ....
7 Juan is Spanish. He's from Granada in ....

3 Write the numbers or dates.

1 My telephone number is oh seven six nine five three double-two one.

2 My date of birth is the twenty-fifth of July two thousand and two.

3 I'm twenty-one years old.

4 The Paris Olympics is in two thousand and twenty-four.

5 I live at two hundred and ninety Green Street.

6 My postcode is S, W, fourteen, eight G, M.

4 Complete the sentences with the words and phrases in the box.

| DOB | driving licence | first name |
| identity card | passport | surname |

1 When you drive a car, you need to have a ....
2 When you enter another country, you usually need to show your .... It is a little book.
3 In some countries people have a(n) .... This shows your photo, your name and your date of birth.
4 Thomas is the .... of a very famous footballer. His .... is Müller.
5 .... means 'Date of Birth'.

GRAMMAR

1 Here are three parts of a conversation, A, B and C. The sentences are in the wrong order. Complete the sentences with the correct form of *be*. Then number the sentences in each part in the correct order.

A
☐ Yes, I ....
☐ Hello, Claudia. I .... Jang.
☐ .... you a new student here, Jang?
☐ Hi! My name .... Claudia.

B
☐ No, we .... We .... from Germany.
☐ Where .... you from, Jang?
☐ I .... from Chengdu, in China. .... you and your family English, Claudia?

C
☐ It .... next to the school café.
☐ No, it .... My teacher's name .... Mrs Rivers.
☐ Oh. So we .... in different classes. Where .... your classroom?
☐ What's your teacher's name, Jang? .... it Mr Johnson?

2 Complete the sentences. Use possessive *'s* or *'s/is*.

0 Jan lives in a small flat.
Jan's flat's / flat is small.

1 Tanya and Nina are sisters. Nina is .... sister.

2 Mike has got a black bag. .... bag is black.

3 Nihal has got an American English teacher. .... English teacher is American.

4 I am Naomi Calder. My .... Naomi Calder.

5 Nick has got an old car. .... old.

3 Read about Dean. Write sentences with *have/has got* or *haven't/hasn't got*.

I'm Dean. I'm studying to be a mechanic at college and I work in a shop at weekends. I live with my parents and my brother Tim in a small flat. We love riding our motorbikes when we have some free time. I don't need a car!

0 (Dean/a job) *Dean has got a job.*
1 (Dean/brother) _____
2 (Dean's parents/sons) _____
3 (Dean's parents/big house) _____
4 (Dean/motorbike) _____
5 (Dean/car) _____

4 Write sentences about Carla and Roberto. Use *can* and *can't*.

	CARLA	ROBERTO
swim one kilometre	✓	✗
speak Spanish	✓	✓
cook paella	✗	✓
write computer programs	✓	✓

1 Carla _____ .
2 Roberto _____ .
3 Roberto and Carla _____ .
4 Carla _____ .
5 Roberto _____ .
6 Roberto and Carla _____ .

5 Complete the conversation about Jill's friend Tomi with the present simple form of the verbs in the box. You need to use some verbs more than once.

come	live	love	speak	work

Davide: Where ¹_____ Tomi _____ from, Jill?
Jill: Japan. But he ²_____ there now. He ³_____ in New York.
Davide: ⁴_____ there too?
Jill: Yes, he ⁵_____ . He ⁶_____ in a language school. He's a teacher.
Davide: Oh, great. Does he teach Japanese?
Jill: No, he ⁷_____ . He teaches Italian.
Davide: ⁸_____ any other languages?
Jill: Yes, he speaks French, too. He ⁹_____ languages!

LISTENING

1  02 Listen and write the letters of the alphabet.

1 _____   **2** _____

2 Put the letters in order to spell two nationalities. What are they?

1 _____   **2** _____

3 03 Listen and write the dates, for example, *15 January 2003.*

1 _____   **3** _____
2 _____   **4** _____

4 04 Read the form for new students at an art school. Then listen and complete the form.

The Art School	Form for new students
Evening course:	¹_____ writing
First name:	²_____
Surname:	³_____
DOB:	⁴_____ 2001
Nationality:	⁵_____
Address:	⁶_____ Road
Phone number:	⁷_____

READING

1 Read about a chef. Put the missing sentences (A–D) in the correct place.

Gabriela Càmara is one of the best chefs in San Francisco, USA. She was born in Mexico and her father is Mexican, but her mother comes from Italy. **1**_____ She lives some of the time in the USA and some of the time in Mexico. **2**_____ Her most famous restaurants are Cala in San Francisco and Contramar in Mexico City. Contramar is 20 years old now, but Cala is only four.

Gabriela started cooking when she was eight. **3**_____ She uses a lot of fish and fresh vegetables in her dishes. Gabriela loves art, so her restaurants are also beautiful places to spend an afternoon or evening. **4**_____ For her, food means spending happy times cooking and eating with her family.

A Now, she makes Mexican food for customers in her restaurants.
B So Gabriela can speak Italian, as well as Spanish and English.
C But most of all, Gabriela loves food.
D This is because she has restaurants in both these countries.

2 Read the text again and write one-word answers.

1 Which country does Gabriela come from? ....
2 What is her mother's nationality? ....
3 Which country is her restaurant Cala in? ....
4 How old is her restaurant Contramar? ....
5 What food does Gabriela cook in her restaurants? vegetables and ....
6 What does Gabriela love? food and ....

SPEAKING

1 Choose the best answers for these statements or questions.

1 Hello.
   - **A** Goodbye.
   - **B** No, thanks.
   - **C** Hi.
2 Nice to meet you.
   - **A** Yes, it is.
   - **B** At the restaurant.
   - **C** Nice to meet you, too.
3 Where do you come from?
   - **A** France. What about you?
   - **B** The swimming pool, I think.
   - **C** In London. Do you know it?
4 Are you married?
   - **A** No, I'm a teacher.
   - **B** No, I'm single.
   - **C** No, I'm Italian.
5 Whose jacket is this?
   - **A** It's a short jacket.
   - **B** It's Harry's.
   - **C** John's got it.
6 How do you spell your surname, please?
   - **A** Kate Lawson.
   - **B** My name's John.
   - **C** It's G-R-A-Y-S-O-N.

2 Write the questions (Q) and answers (A) in the correct place in the table.

I'm twenty.   I'm an actor.
How many brothers and sisters have you got?
What's your first name?   Where do you live?
One of each.   Where do you come from?
In Paris, France.   Patricia.   I'm Italian.
What's your job?   How old are you?

Name
1 Q: .... ?
   A: ....
Age
2 Q: .... ?
   A: ....
Work
3 Q: .... ?
   A: ....
Nationality
4 Q: .... ?
   A: ....
Family
5 Q: .... ?
   A: ....
Home
6 Q: .... ?
   A: ....

WRITING

Complete the profile with *can*, the present simple, *to be* and *has got*.

This is a famous sports person. His first name
¹ .... Cesc. He ² .... two surnames:
Fàbregas and Soler. He ³ .... a footballer
from Spain. At the moment he ⁴ .... in Spain –
he lives in another country. He ⁵ .... four
languages. These are Spanish, Catalan, English
and French. He ⁶ .... married and he
⁷ .... two daughters and one son.

1 A BUSY LIFE

VOCABULARY

1 Complete the sentences with the verbs in the box. You need to use one verb more than once.

> get dressed   get on   get up   have
> put on   stay   take off   wake up

Every weekday, I **¹**_____ at 7.30 and then I **²**_____ in bed for about 15 minutes. At 7.45, I am ready to **³**_____ . I **⁴**_____ a shower and then I **⁵**_____ in a T-shirt and shorts. I **⁶**_____ a quick breakfast, then I **⁷**_____ my bike and cycle to college. There, I **⁸**_____ my T-shirt and shorts and I **⁹**_____ a shirt and jeans.

2 Read the text in Exercise 1 again. Complete the sentences with *after* or *before*.

1 He gets up _____ he wakes up.
2 He stays in bed for 15 minutes _____ he gets up.
3 He has a shower _____ he gets dressed.
4 He has breakfast _____ he puts on his T-shirt and shorts.
5 He rides to work _____ he has breakfast.
6 He takes off his shorts and T-shirt _____ he puts on his shirt and jeans.

3 Write the times. Use *quarter, half* or *o'clock*.

1 **04:45** _____
2 **18:15** _____
3 **11:00** _____
4 **13:30** _____

4 Match the information about the people's work (1–6) with the jobs (a–f).

1 I go to work at an airport and then fly planes.

2 I use a camera every day at work.

3 I repair cars, lorries and motorbikes.

4 I work in an office. I write things in computer language.

5 I help people find things they want to buy.

6 I spend some time in an office and some time in the street. I help people with problems and try to keep them safe.

a a police officer _____
b a mechanic _____
c a photographer _____
d a computer programmer _____
e a pilot _____
f a shop assistant _____

GRAMMAR

1 Complete the text with the correct form of the verbs in brackets. Use the negative form if necessary.

My name is Natalie and my sister's name is Mischa. We **¹**_____ (be) very different. Mischa **²**_____ (work) in a restaurant and I **³**_____ (be) a mechanic. We both **⁴**_____ (start) work at half past eight, but we **⁵**_____ (not get up) at the same time. I always **⁶**_____ (get up) at seven o'clock, but Mischa **⁷**_____ (not like) early mornings – she always stays in bed until eight o'clock. I **⁸**_____ (have) tea and cereal for breakfast, but Mischa **⁹**_____ (not eat) or drink anything at home. She **¹⁰**_____ (have) breakfast later in the morning at work.

2 Read Exercise 1 again. Write yes/no questions about Mischa and Natalie.

0 *Do the sisters start* work at the same time?
   Yes, they do.
1 _____ in a restaurant?
   No, she doesn't.
2 _____ at the same time?
   No, they don't.
3 _____ early mornings?
   No, she doesn't.
4 _____ in bed until eight o'clock?
   Yes, she does.
5 _____ breakfast together?
   No, they don't.
6 _____ tea and cereal for breakfast?
   Yes, she does.

3 Read the table. Then choose the correct answers to complete the sentences about Fran.

HOW OFTEN DO YOU ...	FRAN
go clothes shopping?	one Friday each month
go to the countryside?	every Saturday
spend some time alone?	every evening
play basketball?	every Monday and Thursday
go to a fast-food restaurant?	0 times a year
watch TV?	every Friday, Saturday and Sunday evening

1 On Fridays, Fran _____ goes clothes shopping.
   A usually **B** always **C** sometimes
2 Fran goes to the countryside _____ a week.
   A once **B** twice **C** seven times
3 In the evening, Fran _____ spends some time alone.
   A never **B** often **C** always
4 Fran plays basketball _____ a week.
   A once **B** twice **C** three times
5 Fran _____ goes to a fast food restaurant.
   A never **B** usually **C** always
6 Fran watches TV _____ a week.
   A once **B** twice **C** three times

4 Complete the questions and answers with the correct form of *want* and the verb in brackets.

1 **A:** What _____ you _____ after college? (do)
   B: I _____ to university. (go)
2 **A:** Why _____ Leona _____ a pilot? (be)
   B: Because she _____ around the world. (travel)
3 **A:** What kind of work _____ Billy _____ ? (do)
   B: He _____ a job! He _____ lots of money instead! (not/get, win)
4 **A:** Where _____ Paul and Sophia _____ in Italy? (work)
   B: They _____ on an olive farm. (work)

5 Write sentences about what the people like (👍), love (😍), don't like (👎) or hate (😣).

0 Jane / meet friends for coffee on Saturdays / 😍
   Jane loves meeting friends for coffee on Saturdays.
1 Stefi / go out dancing on Friday evenings / 👍
   ....
2 Louis / stay in bed after he wakes up / 👎
   ....
3 Leo and Tom / play computer games together / 👍
   ....
4 My mum and I / swim in the sea / 😍
   ....
5 Johnnie / go shopping at the supermarket / 😣
   ....
6 My English teacher / work in hot weather / 👎
   ....

LISTENING

1 🎧 05 Listen to two fashion journalists describing their day working at home, and number the sentences 1–6 in the order they do them.

	KENNY	ZADIE
A I start work.		
B I have a hot drink.		
C I get up.	*1*	
D I go for a walk.		
E I spend time talking to people.		
F I go swimming.		

2 🎧 05 Which person are these sentences true for? Can you remember? Circle your answers, then listen again to check.

0 Kenny/(Zadie) walks on the beach every morning.
1 Kenny/Zadie swims in a pool.
2 Kenny/Zadie is married.
3 Kenny/Zadie has a dog.
4 Kenny/Zadie likes drinking green tea.
5 Kenny/Zadie talks to his/her family every day.

Read the texts, then for each question choose the correct answer.

		HEIDI	EVAN	LUCY
1	Which person does some exercise after work?	A	B	C
2	Which person finishes work in the afternoon?	A	B	C
3	Which person takes things to eat to work?	A	B	C
4	Which person travels to and from the airport in different ways?	A	B	C
5	Which person goes to the airport by car?	A	B	C
6	Which person finishes work in the morning?	A	B	C
7	Which person doesn't go home after work every day?	A	B	C

BEING A PILOT *Three pilots tell us about a day at work.*

A Heidi

My first flight is at one o'clock in the afternoon, so I don't get up until 8.30 a.m. I go for a run if I have time, have a shower and put on my uniform. I put all the food and water I need for the day in my flight bag and I leave the house on my bike. Sometimes I have a long flight, and I can't come home for two or three days, but I usually fly to Germany, Poland, the UK and France.

B Evan

I work for five days and then I don't work for four days after that. On work mornings, my alarm clock wakes me up at quarter to four. I drink a cup of tea in bed, have a shower and drive to the airport. I meet my team for the day, and then we fly two or sometimes three flights. I drive home at about three o'clock and I always feel really tired so I never stay up late in the evening after work.

C Lucy

I leave home in the afternoon, about three hours before my 4.00 p.m. flight. I take the bus to the airport. Before I get on the plane, I meet my flight team, and we eat sandwiches while we talk. We fly all night, but I can sleep for about three hours on the plane. We arrive back here at 7.00 a.m. and I get home by taxi an hour later. I have breakfast, go to the gym, and then sleep before work.

PUSH YOURSELF B1

Read the job advert, then tick the correct sentences and cross the wrong sentences.

Shop Assistant
Hartog's Books

We need a new shop assistant to join the small team of four employees at our book store in New Street

£23,000–25,000 a year
No experience needed

Email your CV to
hartogbks@network1.com
Interviews with shop manager 3rd May

📞 For further information call 0789 435680

1 The text does not give any information about the shop assistant's salary. ☐
2 You can only do the job if you have been a shop assistant before. ☐
3 You have to send your CV. ☐
4 The shop manager wants to see all new shop assistants on 3rd May. ☐
5 Four other people work at the shop. ☐

Read the information about Ismail. Write five questions to ask him and then write his answers.

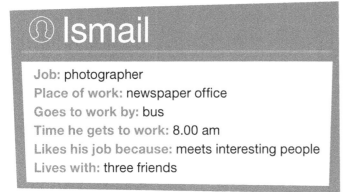

Ismail

Job: photographer
Place of work: newspaper office
Goes to work by: bus
Time he gets to work: 8.00 am
Likes his job because: meets interesting people
Lives with: three friends

0 Q: What *(job) do you do?*
   A: *I'm a photographer.*
1 Q: Where _____ ?
   A: _____
2 Q: How _____ ?
   A: _____
3 Q: When _____ ?
   A: _____
4 Q: Why _____ ?
   A: _____
5 Q: Who _____ ?
   A: _____

Write the beginnings and endings of emails in the correct places in the emails.

| Dear | Hi | Love from | the best | wishes |

To: Mr Thomas
From: Billy Harmer
Reply Forward

¹ _____ Mr Thomas,

I was ill yesterday and so I did not come to the English lesson. Could you tell me what the homework is for this week?

Best ² _____
Billy Harmer

To: Grandma
From: Celine
Reply Forward

³ _____ Grandma,

Can I visit you tomorrow at about 3 pm? I'd like to come after work – we finish early tomorrow.

⁴ _____ , Celine

To: John
From: Sam
Reply Forward

Hello John,

I hope you are OK. Could you send me the information about the college trip, please? I didn't get the email about it.

Thanks.

All ⁵ _____ , Sam

2 CHANGING WORLD

VOCABULARY

1 Complete the sentences with the name of the month.

1 .... is the first month of the year.
2 August is the month before ....
3 .... is the seventh month of the year.
4 .... is between February and April.
5 The month after May is ....
6 .... is between September and November.
7 The last month of the year is ....

2 Write the seasons for Melbourne, Australia.

Melbourne's seasons are the opposite of the UK's.

	THE UK	MELBOURNE
December – February	winter	1 ....
March – May	spring	2 ....
June – August	summer	3 ....
September – November	autumn	4 ....

3 Complete the sentences with the words in the box. You need to change some words into adjectives.

| cloud fog ice lightning rain |
| snow storm sun temperature |

1 In very cold winters, you can walk on the .... on the lake.
2 It will be a .... night tonight, with thunder and ....
3 The .... in summer is usually between 20 and 28 °C.
4 It's hot but there's a large grey .... in the sky, so we'll have some .... later, I think.
5 On .... days in the summer, we don't go outside because it's too hot.
6 It's warm today but it was .... this morning, so it was difficult to see across the street.
7 People like .... weather because the white trees and countryside look beautiful.

4 Label the photos with the words in the box.

| a coast a desert a forest an island |
| a lake a mountain a valley a waterfall |

A

....

B

....

C

....

D

....

E

....

F

....

G

....

H

....

1 Complete the text with the present continuous form of the verbs in brackets. Make the verb negative if necessary.

Today it's really cold so I ¹_____ (wear) lots of warm clothes. It's icy outside and it ²_____ (snow), too. I'm sitting in the library at college with some friends, but we ³_____ (study) – we ⁴_____ (talk) about going home early in case the buses stop because of the snow! My friends Freddie and Lena live in the hills so they ⁵_____ (leave) now, but Karin and Graham ⁶_____ (go) home now because they live very near and can easily walk home in the snow.

2 Write the questions and answers to make a conversation.

Mike: Hi Laurence, I can't come to tennis practice tonight – I'm not at home. I'm in Birmingham.

Laurence: What / do / there?
¹_____

Mike: I'm here with my team. We / work here / this week. ²_____

Laurence: Stay / in a hotel? ³_____

Mike: Yes, a really nice one. I / have / a great week!
⁴_____
How about you?

Laurence: I'm on holiday this week. So I / not work.
⁵_____

Mike: Great! Where / stay?
⁶_____

Laurence: At home. Some friends / visit us / at the moment.
⁷_____

Mike: That's nice. Have a good week.

3 Complete the sentences with the present continuous or present simple form of the verbs in brackets.

1 It is 7.30 am, and I _____ breakfast. I usually _____ it at 7.00, but I'm late today. (have)

2 Cathy always _____ family parties, so she _____ her grandmother's birthday meal this afternoon very much. (enjoy)

3 Usually, Harry _____ only with his parents, but at the moment his cousin _____ with them because she has a summer job in their town. (live)

4 Ali and his friends _____ football in the park this morning. They _____ there three or four times a week. (play)

5 Gregorio is a taxi driver. He _____ a taxi in London. But this week he _____ across France because he is on holiday. (drive)

6 In the summer it _____ a lot in my country, and it's very hot. It _____ today. (rain)

1 Read the text and choose the best title for it.

A Why I will never leave Ascension Island
B Living and working on Ascension Island
C Remembering my time on Ascension Island

I'm Marcus Higgs and I'm a conservation officer. This means I work in the countryside, and I look after the animals and plants that live there. I was born in Devon, in the south of England, but at the moment I am living and working on Ascension Island. Ascension Island is in the middle of the ocean between Africa and South America. I am here for two years.

I work in a beautiful place called the Green Mountain National Park. In the park, there is a mountain and some hills, and there are some smaller islands in the water around the coast, and lots of beaches of course. I work on projects to make these places better for plants and animals. There are lots of interesting sea animals and birds here, and the conservation team are working hard to keep them safe. I also give information to visitors to the island and tell them about our projects.

This week, we are putting some new trees around our visitor centre. I love my job here, but living on Ascension Island is not always easy. Only 800 people live here, and there is only one restaurant! But I am enjoying the weather – the temperature is 25–34 °C all year – and I have lots of new American friends.

2 Complete the sentences with one or two words from the text.

1 What is Marcus's job? – He's a _____ .

2 Which part of England does Marcus come from? – He's from the _____ of the country.

3 Which continents is Marcus living nearest? – He is living nearest to _____ and _____ .

4 What can you see near the coast of Green Mountain National Park? – There are some _____ .

5 Who does Marcus help at work? He helps _____ .

6 What does Marcus like about Ascension Island? He likes his new friends, his job and _____ .

Choose the correct adjectives to complete the sentences.

1 We had *strong/heavy* snow yesterday morning, and the children had lots of fun playing in it in the afternoon.
2 The winds are really *strong/hard* this morning so our plane can't leave.
3 When the fog is *thick/heavy* on the coast, the fishing boats do not go out to sea.
4 We had a great walk up the mountain in *high/bright* sunshine all the way to the top. There were *clear/empty* skies all day.
5 We have a lot of *hard/strong* frosts in winter in the north of the country.

LISTENING PART 1

 06 **For each question, choose the correct answer.**

1 What weather does Maria's island usually have in March?

A  B  C

2 Where is the man's uncle travelling now?

A 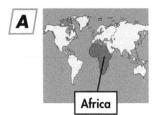 B 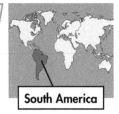 C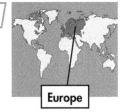

Africa   South America   Europe

3 What is Jessica's friend, Lucy, doing in the forest?

A  B  C

4 Where is Richard working this week?

A  B  C

5 In which month does Monica stay with her grandparents?

A B  C

SPEAKING

1 Look at the photo and choose the correct options.

1 In the photo, *there's/it's* a family on a snowy mountain.
2 *Maybe/Actually* they are on holiday.
3 The parents are *sitting/walking* at the top of the mountain and the children are playing.
4 Two children are *on the right/in the middle* of the photo.
5 There's a lot of snow on the mountain, but at the moment *there's/it's* sunny.
6 I think they *are enjoying/enjoy* their day on the mountain.
7 The children and the parents *don't wear/aren't wearing* helmets. That would be a good idea.
8 I can *see/seeing* some clouds in the sky.
9 There is a lake *below/above* the mountains.

2 Write the number of the sentence in the correct box. For some boxes two numbers are possible.

What is there in the photo? Sentence number:	Describing details Sentence number: ....
What is happening in the photo? Sentence number:	The weather in the photo Sentence number: ....
Where are things in the photo? Sentence number:	What do you think? Sentence number: ....

WRITING

1 Read the email and underline the three ways of inviting someone to do something.

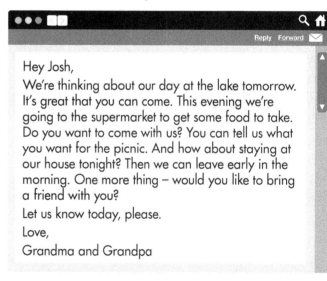

Hey Josh,

We're thinking about our day at the lake tomorrow. It's great that you can come. This evening we're going to the supermarket to get some food to take. Do you want to come with us? You can tell us what you want for the picnic. And how about staying at our house tonight? Then we can leave early in the morning. One more thing – would you like to bring a friend with you?

Let us know today, please.

Love,

Grandma and Grandpa

2 Put the words in order to make Josh's possible answers to the invitation.

1 I've got / from 4 pm–6.30 pm. / but I'm afraid / I'd / football practice / love to come

....

2 be / That / wonderful. / would

....

3 are / but / for asking / busy / Thanks / tomorrow. / friends / my / all

....

3 FREE TIME, SCREEN TIME?

VOCABULARY

1 Complete the paragraphs with the words in the box.

blogger	comments	download	episode
series	social media	stream	upload

Blogs

A ¹_____ is someone who writes on a kind of online site called a blog. He or she needs to ²_____ new articles or videos onto this site very often, so people will visit it a lot. People follow blogs that they find on ³_____ and they can post ⁴_____ about the blogs if they want to.

Watching films and TV programmes

If you really enjoy a ⁵_____ of TV programmes, you can go online and buy one ⁶_____ from it, or all of them. Some TV channels have a website where you can get their programmes in two ways. If you want to get a programme to watch later, you can ⁷_____ it, or you can watch it immediately if you ⁸_____ it from the website.

2 Complete the TV listings page with the types of programme in the box. There are 2 words you do not need.

action film	cartoon	comedy	crime drama
documentary	horror	news	quiz show

3 Match the words (1–5) with the details about the film (a–e). What kind of film is it?

1 the setting ☐   4 the plot ☐
2 a dialogue ☐   5 a scene ☐
3 the characters ☐

a They are in a huge city on Mars.
b They are on Mars, but have to get back to Earth to find something that will save Mars.
c They are called Leona, Sheena, Marvin and Bennie.
d Leona and Marvin are sitting in a Martian kitchen. They're planning their journey.
e *Leona:* Mars needs us.
Marvin: And we need Mars.

GRAMMAR

1 Complete the sentences with the past simple form of *be*. Sometimes you need the negative form.

1 My friends and I went to the park last night. We _____ there until about 9.00 pm.
2 Eva _____ at the concert yesterday. She went to the cinema.
3 _____ you at the match yesterday? There _____ some great goals!
4 Who _____ your English teacher last year?
5 There _____ many people at the party because Hugh only invited a few of his friends.
6 Which classroom _____ you in this morning?

Channel 19		Evening programmes
6.00	Find out what's happened today from our journalists around the world	¹ _____
6.45	Learn about the flowers in the forests of South America	² _____
7.45	Police officer Rachel Kinsella (actor, Amy Black) finds a body in the river	³ _____
8.45	Watch TV stars doing funny things to make you laugh	⁴ _____
9.45	Two teams of TV stars answer questions about the world this year	⁵ _____
10.15	Made in 2018, this is an exciting, fast-moving story of a woman trying to find her husband before it's too late	⁶ _____

2 Complete the conversations with the past simple form of the verbs in the box.
Sometimes you need the negative form.

| decide | enjoy | finish | help |
| love | play | watch | work |

1 **A:** .... you .... the football on TV last night?

   B: No, I .... some games online.

2 **A:** Where .... your friends .... to go for dinner?

   B: The Old Ship restaurant. They .... it there.

3 **A:** What time .... you .... work today?

   B: At lunchtime. I .... this afternoon.

4 **A:** I .... Grandma to make some bread at the weekend.

   B: .... you .... doing that?

3 Complete the sentences about Amanda's week.

LAST TUESDAY	SUNDAY AM	MONDAY AM	TUESDAY AM
go shopping	get up / 10 o'clock	speak / uncle	have breakfast / café
			TUESDAY PM
			now

1 Amanda .... yesterday.

2 Amanda .... a week ago.

3 Amanda .... the day before yesterday.

4 Amanda .... this morning.

READING PART 3

For each question, choose the correct answer.

1 What do we learn about Helena in the first paragraph?

   A Her blog is for visitors to New York.

   B She writes a blog every weekend.

   C Writing a blog is not her only job.

2 How long are most of Helena's trips?

   A one day

   B two days

   C four days

3 Helena decided to go to Morocco because

   A her friends told her about it.

   B she saw something on television about it.

   C she read about it online.

4 Helena thinks people read her blog because

   A they believe what she writes.

   B they like her.

   C they enjoy the way she writes.

5 What is the last paragraph about?

   A the advice someone gave Helena

   B Helena's hopes for the future

   C what Helena wants her blog to do

Helena Cooper's life as a blogger

When she was young, Helena Cooper was very ill. She is better now and wants to spend her free time doing interesting things. Helena has two jobs: she works three days a week in Chicago, USA, and she is also a travel blogger. Her blog shows that you can travel the world at the weekend, and it doesn't need to cost too much.

For most people a 'weekend' is two days, but Helena's trips are usually four. Sometimes she only goes for one day, and she even went to Austria once for nine hours!

Her first trip was to Morocco. She watched a TV programme about it, and started to look for flights and hotels online. Helena's friends thought she was silly to go for just a few days, but that didn't stop her.

When she came back, everyone asked her lots of questions about Morocco, and she answered the same questions many times. So she wrote them down, and started her blog. She gives information only about the places she visits, so people know it is right. Helena thinks this is why people follow her blog and like it.

Helena writes about the places she visits, but she doesn't want everyone to do the same things as her. She also thinks people shouldn't wait to do the things they really want to do. Her blog tries to show people that they *can* do those things *now*!

PUSH YOURSELF /B1

1 Circle two correct answers in each sentence.

1 A good film is *dull/enjoyable/amusing*.
2 A funny film is *amusing/silly/serious*.
3 A bad film is *awful/brilliant/disappointing*.
4 A boring film is *scary/dull/uninteresting*.

2 Are the sentences true (T) or false (F)?

1 Horror films are usually scary. ....
2 Cartoons are usually serious. ....
3 Crime dramas are usually silly. ....
4 Documentary films are usually amusing. ....
5 Nature films are usually serious. ....

LISTENING

1 07 **Listen and number the topics (A–D) in the order you hear them.**

A an outside activity ☐
B doing something with family members ☐
C the weather on Saturday ☐
D different kinds of TV ☐

2 07 **Who are the sentences true for, Ryan or Anna? Listen again and circle the correct answer.**

1 *Ryan/Anna* was in the city on Saturday.
2 *Ryan/Anna* downloaded a science fiction TV series.
3 *Ryan/Anna* enjoys watching crime drama programmes.
4 *Ryan/Anna* enjoyed playing a video game.
5 *Ryan/Anna* played a game with a parent.
6 *Ryan/Anna* met some friends.

SPEAKING

1 Write the words in the correct order to make questions.

1 weekend / How / your / was

_____?

2 last / get / What / you / to / night / did / up

_____?

3 a / you / good / have / weekend / Did

_____?

4 Friday / on / do / afternoons / do / What / you

_____?

5 usually / you / shopping / Do / go / Saturdays / on

_____?

2 Match the answers (A–E) with the questions (1–5) in Exercise 1.

A I visit my family in our village. ☐
B No, I go on Monday evenings. ☐
C No, it was terrible! ☐
D It was really good, thanks. ☐
E Not much. I had a quiet evening. ☐

3 Put the missing 'follow-up' questions (a–d) in the correct place.

a Do you often go walking?
b Did you walk a long way?
c How often do you have to do that?
d What kind of food did you take?

Cathy: I went for a picnic in the forest on Saturday.
Elena: That's nice. ¹_____
Cathy: Lots of salad and cold meat. We went for a lovely walk after our meal, too.
Elena: ²_____
Cathy: We walked about five kilometres, from the visitor centre to the lake.
Elena: ³_____
Cathy: Yes, when I'm not working at the weekend.
Elena: ⁴_____
Cathy: One weekend a month.

WRITING

Complete the sentences with the correct beginnings in the box.

> My favourite character is   My favourite moment is
> The best things about the film are   The plot is
> The setting is   The story is about

1 _____ a castle. It's in the mountains.

2 _____ a group of students who get lost in the mountains. It's a bit silly really.

3 _____ very easy to follow.

4 _____ Marlon, because he's so funny. The others are good too, but he is the best.

5 _____ when Marlon finds a donkey and he tries to ride it!

6 _____ the actors and the dialogue. They're brilliant.

4 KEEP FIT, FEEL GOOD

VOCABULARY

1 **Are the sentences true (T) or false (F)? Correct the false sentences.**

1 You have six toes on each foot. ....

2 Your neck is between your head and your body.
....

3 Your heart is inside your body. ....

4 When you eat, the food goes into your stomach.
....

5 Your back is below your head. ....

6 Your knees are in the middle of your arms. ....

7 Your brain is inside your head. ....

8 Your fingers are part of your face. ....

2 **Complete the sentences with words from Exercise 1.**

1 You use your .... for thinking.

2 You use your .... for turning your head.

3 You use your .... for playing the piano.

4 You use your .... for carrying a backpack.

5 You use your .... to stand up.

3 **Choose the correct words to complete the sentences.**

1 Why is Ellie going to see her .... ?
Because she has ....
(*toothache/doctor/ambulance/dentist*)

2 Where did you buy this .... ?
From the ....
(*back/medicine/pharmacy/ache*)

3 Is Jennie still feeling .... ?
No, she feels .... now.
(*broken/hurt/sick/fine*)

4 Why is Lara at the .... ?
Because she broke her ....
(*leg/medicine/hospital/dentist*)

GRAMMAR

1 **Read the information and complete the sentences with *can, can't, could* or *couldn't*.**

Leah is 20 years old now.

Can Leah …	
ride a horse?	Yes. She learned when she was 10.
cook a nice meal?	Yes. She learned when she was 16.
swim 1,000 metres?	No.
speak Chinese?	Yes. She learned when she was 13.
drive a car?	No.
ride a motorbike?	Yes. She learned when she was 17.

1 Leah .... ride a horse now.

2 Leah .... ride a horse when she was nine.

3 Leah .... speak Chinese when she was 18.

4 Leah .... swim 1000 metres now.

5 Leah .... cook a nice meal when she was 12.

6 Leah .... ride a motorbike when she was 18.

2 **Write questions about Leah for these answers.**

1 .... ? Yes, she can. She learned three years ago.

2 .... ? No, she can't.

3 .... when she was 12? Yes, she could.

4 .... when she was 19? No, she couldn't.

3 Complete the sentences with *should* or *shouldn't*.

Be a good sleeper!

1. You .... watch an exciting film just before you go to bed.
2. You .... turn off your phone about an hour before you go to bed.
3. You .... eat a big meal late in the evening.
4. You .... write down anything you are worried about before going to sleep. This helps you to stop worrying.
5. You .... try to go to bed at the same time every night.
6. You .... sleep a lot in the day.
7. You .... do some exercise every day.
8. .... I stay in bed if I can't sleep? – No, get up and have a hot drink.

PUSH YOURSELF B1

Answer the questions with the correct part of the body in the box.

ankle	elbow	hips	lungs	muscles	wrist

1. Where do you wear a bracelet? ....
2. What get bigger when air goes into them? ....
3. What joins the foot and the leg? ....
4. What bones are at the top of legs? ....
5. What is about half way between your shoulder and your hand? ....
6. What get larger when you exercise a lot? ....

LISTENING PART 2

 08 For each question, write the correct answer in the gap. Write one word or a number or a date or a time.

You will hear the secretary of a running club telling new members about the club.

Hodd Town Running Club

Secretary's name:	Daniella Black
Day club meets:	**(1)** ....
Meeting time this month:	**(2)** .... p.m.
Beginners' runs:	**(3)** .... kilometres
Place for dry weather runs:	the **(4)** ....
Special day, 18 June:	a **(5)** .... at Jack's Hill

READING

1 **Read the text and choose the two correct answers.**

What happened in *all* the stories?

A Someone fell off something.
B There was an animal.
C Something happened to a child.
D Someone broke a bone.
E Someone went to hospital.

SILLY ACCIDENTS

CINDY

When I was young, I loved a film about an elephant that could fly. One day, I went into my brother's room and climbed up to my brother's bed. It was about two metres high. I decided to try to fly like the elephant, so I jumped off the bed. I couldn't fly of course – I fell to the floor and then my mum came into the room. She took me to hospital, and we learned my foot was broken.

JONELLE

I was at my desk in my office when an insect came in through an open window. I tried to climb up onto the desk because I wanted to kill the insect, but I fell and hit my hand on the chair. It hurt a lot, and a friend took me to the hospital, where the doctor told me one of my fingers was broken.

DAVID

Last summer, I took a friend's dog for a walk. I love this dog because it's friendly and does funny things, but it's also large and heavy. I walked across a field, and the dog ran around, having a great time. I stopped to watch the dog, but then it ran straight at me and bumped into the top of my left leg really hard. I had to go to the hospital in an ambulance, where they found my leg was broken.

ANTONIO

I broke my wrist two years ago. It was just before a football match. I put my football things into my big sports bag, and then my cat came into my bedroom with a frog in its mouth! There are lots of frogs in the fields near my house. The frog jumped all around my bedroom, but I didn't want to pick it up in my hands. I got a towel, put it over the frog and picked it up. But then I didn't see my sports bag and fell over it. My arm and hand really hurt after that, and my dad took me to hospital.

2 **Write one word from the text to complete the sentences.**

1 Cindy tried to _____ after she watched a film.
2 Cindy broke her _____ .
3 Jonelle was in her _____ when an insect flew in.
4 Jonelle broke her _____ .
5 David stood in a _____ and watched a dog.
6 David broke his _____ .
7 Antonio used a _____ to catch the frog.
8 Antonio broke his _____ .

1 Complete the conversation with the correct phrase in the box.

| Are you OK?   better   How are you? |
| how's   sorry to hear that   What's the matter |

Leanne: Hi, Natalie, I heard you had an accident on your bike last week. **¹** ....

Natalie: Yes, thanks. I hurt my arm and my ankle, but my arm's **²** .... now.

Leanne: That's good. But **³** .... your ankle?

Natalie: It still hurts a bit. What about you? **⁴** ....

Leanne: Not bad, thanks. But I've got a problem with my shoulder.

Natalie: I'm **⁵** .... **⁶** .... with it?

Leanne: I hurt it in a game of tennis, so I'm resting it. It will be fine soon.

Natalie: I hope so!

2 Match the problems (1–6) with the advice (a–f).

1 I want to be a lorry driver, but I can't drive!
2 I'd like to see a different city.
3 My dad never listens to my ideas.
4 I'd like a pet but I live in a small flat.
5 My teacher always gives me bad marks.
6 I can't decide what colour to paint my kitchen.

a You shouldn't get a dog, but a cat might be OK.
b Why don't you go to Lisbon? It's lovely.
c How about trying a few and seeing which looks best?
d You should learn to.
e How about talking to him about how you can make them better?
f You should ask him why he doesn't.

WRITING

Complete the paragraph with the words and phrases in the box.

| after that   one day   suddenly   then |

Strange
but true!

¹ .... when I was about 10, I was in the supermarket with my mum. We stopped to look at something, and laughed about it, and then **²** .... we heard a strange sound and my foot really started to hurt. My mum said, 'You can't break a foot just standing on it!' so **³** .... we went home. When we got home, Mum looked at my foot again. It looked worse and still hurt a lot. **⁴** .... , Mum took me to hospital and we found out it was broken!

5 MORE THAN A HOLIDAY

VOCABULARY

1 Cross out the wrong word in each set.

1	**Accommodation:**	a comfortable hotel	a tent	a flight
2	**Luggage:**	a traveller	a suitcase	a backpack
3	**Places:**	a campsite	street food	a destination
4	**A travel problem:**	have a delay	miss a bus	catch a train
5	**Travel activity:**	go to work	go on a tour	visit a tourist information centre
6	**People:**	a local family	a tour guide	a national park

2 Complete the sentences with words from Exercise 1.

1 Suitcases and .... are examples of .... you take on holiday.
2 If you .... a train, there will be a .... in your journey.
3 What kind of .... do you prefer on holiday? I like staying in my .... on a nice campsite.
4 If you are not with a ...., go to a .... for advice about places to see.

3 Complete the sentences with the words in the box.

crossing	cruise	flight	journey	travel	trip

1 The car .... from my home to London is about five hours long.
2 Our .... leaves Paris Charles de Gaulle airport at 7.30 pm.
3 Yesterday, we went on a really fun shopping ....
4 I enjoy ...., especially around other countries.
5 My granddad is going on a .... around the Antarctic Ocean for two weeks.
6 I didn't enjoy the .... between the city and the island because the weather was so stormy and the sea was rough.

GRAMMAR

1 Complete the sentences with the past continuous form of the verbs in the box. Use the negative form if necessary.

camp	listen	look	rain	read	watch	win

1 Yesterday, I .... a book all afternoon.
2 The student .... to the teacher so she learned nothing.
3 At nine thirty we .... a documentary about sea animals.
4 .... we .... in France in the summer of 2014?
5 .... it .... in the south west of the country yesterday?
6 They .... at the sea so they didn't see the flying fish.
7 .... you .... your tennis match when I saw you in the park?

2 Complete the sentences with the correct form of the verb. Use the past simple or past continuous.

The afternoon before Martha's holiday

2.30–3.30 sit in the living room and read a guide book	**2.45** book a taxi
3.30–5.00 pack her suitcase	**3.45** find a necklace **4.00** mother calls
5.00–5.45 look for her passport	**5.15** ask her brother to help **5.30** find US dollars

1 Martha .... a guide book when she .... in the living room.
2 Martha .... a taxi at 2.45.
3 Martha .... her suitcase when her mother ....
4 When Martha .... her suitcase, she .... a necklace in it.
5 Martha .... her brother to help when she .... for her passport.
6 When Martha .... for her passport, she .... some US dollars.

READING PART 4

1 Read the text in Exercise 2. Tick the correct paragraph.

		PARAGRAPH 1	PARAGRAPH 2
1	how long the railway is		
2	what you can see from the railway		
3	how you can get to the railway		
4	the most popular trip on the railway		
5	how it got its name		
6	why people visit it		

2 For each question, choose the correct answer.

The Darjeeling Toy Train

The Darjeeling Mountain Railway in north-east India is called the 'Toy Train' because its trains are so small. It is nearly 140 years old and is **1** .... with tourists because it's in a very beautiful mountain area. It also has the highest station in India (2,225.7 metres) and from some places, there are fantastic **2** .... of the world's third highest mountain, Kanchenjunga.

The railway is 88 kilometres **3** ...., going between New Jalpaiguri station and Darjeeling town. The trains are very slow, and the whole **4** .... takes about eight hours, so most tourists **5** .... a shorter, two-hour trip from Darjeeling to Ghoom and back again. Lots of people go on these trips as part of a tour of India. You can get a **6** .... from Delhi or Calcutta to the railway's nearest airport, Bagdogra.

1 **A** favourite **B** great **C** popular
2 **A** pictures **B** views **C** shows
3 **A** long **B** far **C** large
4 **A** crossing **B** journey **C** cruise
5 **A** prefer **B** hope **C** need
6 **A** destination **B** travel **C** flight

LISTENING

1 **09 Listen to Daniel talking about a cruise he went on. Number the topics in the order you hear them.**

Topics Daniel talks about

A activities on the cruise ☐
B the other passengers ☐
C why he went on the cruise ☐
D eating on the ship ☐
E the size of the ship ☐

2 **09 Listen again and choose the correct answers to complete each sentence.**

1 Daniel is a
   A cruise company worker.
   B magazine journalist.
   C student of travel and tourism.

2 The cruise began in
   A Italy.
   B Turkey.
   C Greece.

3 Daniel thought the food on the cruise was
   A very good.
   B OK.
   C not interesting.

4 The cruise made Daniel feel
   A bored.
   B worried.
   C tired.

5 Daniel was surprised about how … the people were on the cruise.
   A young
   B friendly
   C like him

Choose the correct phrase to complete the story.

A when I arrived home
B I bumped into a tree in the street
C I met my friend, Paul
D I missed my bus home
E as my mum and I were having dinner
F when Paul drove past me in his car

When I was shopping for some clothes yesterday afternoon, **¹**_____ . While Paul and I were talking, **²**_____ , so I had to walk. I was walking home **³**_____ . While I was waving to him, **⁴**_____ ! I turned red, but luckily none of my friends saw me. My mum was waiting for me **⁵**_____ . Later, **⁶**_____ , I told her about my shopping trip. She thought it was funny!

SPEAKING

1 Match the sentences (1–6) with their meanings (a–f).

1

> The city was full of people so it was really difficult to walk down the streets.

2

> There was no traffic noise and very few people.

3

> After walking in the sun all day, I went to bed early and slept for about nine hours.

4

> It made me feel great: I enjoyed resting and didn't worry about anything.

5

> All the people who visited this place with me really loved it.

6

> You could hear people shouting and police cars in the street all night.

a It was popular.

d It was quiet.

b It was relaxing.

e It was very crowded.

c It was noisy.

f It was tiring.

2 Complete the conversation with the words in the box.

enjoy	fantastic	for me	had	terrible	think

Patricia: Did you **1**_____ your holiday, Lucia?

Lucia: Well, some of it. We loved camping in the mountains. We **2**_____ a great time there and the campsite was **3**_____ – there was a huge swimming pool.

Patricia: That's good. But you didn't like everything about your holiday?

Lucia: No. After the mountains, we travelled to the coast. We hated that because the beaches were **4**_____. They were very crowded and very dirty.

Patricia: Oh no! Were you camping?

Lucia: No, we stayed in a hotel. That was OK, but **5**_____, staying in a hotel is not as exciting as camping. I **6**_____ sleeping in a tent is the best thing about being on holiday!

Patrica: So what did you do?

Lucia: We went back to the campsite!

WRITING

Complete the postcard with the words or phrases in the box.

after that	Right now	the evening	This morning	while	Yesterday

Hi Mum,

I'm having a great holiday with Uncle Ronnie. Today we're visiting the city. **1**_____ we went to the city museum. It was fantastic – there were lots of videos and activities. **2**_____ we're sitting in a restaurant by the river. We had lunch here. Uncle Ronnie is on his phone **3**_____ I'm writing to you.

4_____ afternoon we went to your favourite place – the zoo! We went for a burger **5**_____, and later in **6**_____ we watched films at home.

See you soon,

Tyler

6 TIME FOR FOOD

VOCABULARY

1 Label the photos with the words in the box.

a beef curry   a chicken
a mango   an omelette
some broccoli   some cereal
some mushrooms   some yoghurt

A

B

C

D

E

F

2 Write the words in the box in the correct place on the menu.

Desserts   Dinner   Lunch   Main courses   Starters

G

H

NEW BRIDGE HOTEL
MENU

1 ....
Mushrooms on toast
Tomato salad
Broccoli soup

2 ....
Chicken curry with rice and yoghurt
Potato, mushroom and cheese omelette
Chicken with vegetables and chips
Beef and chilli with rice and green salad

3 ....
Ice cream
Chocolate cake
Fruit

Meal times: **4** .... is 12.00 noon – 2.00 p.m.
    5 .... is 6.00 p.m. – 9.00 p.m.

3 Cross out the wrong word or words in each set.

1 a piece of:
yoghurt   cake   chicken   ice cream

2 a carton of:
cream   milk   chocolate   orange juice

3 a slice of:
bread   soup   cheese   cereal

4 a packet of:
eggs   pasta   biscuits   sweets

GRAMMAR

1 Complete the conversation with *a*, *an*, *some* or *any*.

Lela: What are you doing, Sammi?

Sammi: I'm cooking ¹........... pasta for dinner.

Lela: Can I help?

Sammi: Yes, please. Can you get ²........... cheese from the fridge?

Lela: Mm ... I can't see ³........... cheese in the fridge, Sammi.

Sammi: There's ⁴........... egg box on the top shelf – it's under that.

Lela: Oh yes, I've found it!

Sammi: Are there ⁵........... tomatoes in the fridge?

Lela: Er ... no, I can't find ⁶........... in the fridge. But there's ⁷........... bowl of tomatoes on the table.

Sammi: Oh yes! I forgot about those.

Lela: Would you like ⁸........... drink while you're cooking?

Sammi: I'd love one.

2 Tick the phrases you can use with each kind of food.

	APPLE	RICE	BISCUIT	BURGER	SALT	BREAD
how many	✓					
how much						
a little						
a few	✓					
not much						
not many	✓					
a lot of	✓					

3 Write questions with *How much* / *How many* and answers with *a lot* and *not many* / *not much*.

	MARTIN	NADYA
coffee	9 cups a day	1 cup a day
crisps	about 1 packet a week	3–4 packets a day
meat	every day	once a week
chocolate	1 bar a month	3 bars a day
eggs	2–3 a day	2–3 a week

0 (coffee/Martin)   *How much coffee does Martin drink? – A lot.*

1 (crisps/Nadya)   ....

2 (meat/Nadya)   ....

3 (chocolate/Martin)   ....

4 (eggs/Nadya)   ....

4 Complete the sentences about Nadya with *eat/drink* and *a lot of*, *not many* or *not much*.

1 Nadya .... coffee each day.

2 Nadya .... crisps every day.

3 Nadya .... meat each week.

4 Nadya .... chocolate every day.

5 Nadya .... eggs each week.

LISTENING PART 5

 🔊 10 For each question, choose the correct answer.

You will hear Pippa talking to her friend Mario about desserts in a restaurant. Which dessert does each person want?

Example   Pippa   [F]

PEOPLE		**DESSERTS**	
1 David ☐		**A**	baked pears
2 Mario ☐		**B**	chocolate cake
3 Helen ☐		**C**	coconut rice
4 Sarah ☐		**D**	ice cream
5 Paul ☐		**E**	lemon cake and biscuits
		F	mango
		G	strawberries and cream
		H	yoghurt and honey

PUSH YOURSELF B1

Complete the recipe with the words in the box.

add (x2)	burn	chop	fry
grill	peel (x2)	steam	stir

Spanish omelette

You need:

2 potatoes
1 onion
olive oil
5 large eggs
pepper and salt

- Wash and ¹_____ the potatoes.
- ²_____ them into small pieces.
- ³_____ the onion and then cut it into slices.
- Put some oil into a small frying pan.
- ⁴_____ the onion and potatoes slowly, for about 20 minutes, until the onions are soft and light brown. Do not ⁵_____ them very much or the potatoes will break.
- Put the eggs in a bowl and ⁶_____ some salt and pepper. Stir them well.
- When the onions and potatoes are ready, ⁷_____ them to the eggs.
- Put the eggs, onions and potatoes back in the pan and cook for about 20 minutes. Make sure the bottom of the omelette doesn't ⁸_____ . If the top does not cook, put it in the oven and ⁹_____ it for a few minutes until it's brown.
- When it's ready, put it on a plate and cut it into slices.
- ¹⁰_____ some broccoli over a pan of boiling water and serve that with the hot omelette.

READING

1 Read the text. Choose the best title for it.

- **A** How to take great photos of food
- **B** How the young and old choose food
- **C** How to learn from your mistakes

I went to a restaurant for lunch with my granddad yesterday, and when the starters came, I got out my phone and took some photos of them. My granddad was very surprised, and he laughed at me. 'Food is for eating!' he said. 'Why are you taking photos of it?' Then I was surprised. Didn't he know why?

All my friends take photos of food in restaurants to share on social media, and when we're deciding which restaurant to go to, we look at photos people post on social media. Before I go to a restaurant, I also look at photos on social media to see the food on the menu. So when I arrive at the restaurant, I know what I want to eat.

Yesterday, my granddad chose mushroom soup for his starter because he likes soup, and I chose baked cheese because it looked delicious in a photo I saw on my phone. Both dishes were very good.

We finished our starters and then Granddad looked at the menu for the main course. He couldn't decide between a fish dish and a beef dish. 'Would you like to see some photos of them?' I asked. He laughed again. 'OK,' he said. I got out my phone again, found the photos and gave him the phone. He decided the beef looked nicer because it came with rice and broccoli. The same thing happened with the desserts.

After the meal, I asked Granddad, 'Will you use photos on social media to choose your food next time you eat out?' 'Maybe,' he said. 'If I'm with one of my grandchildren!'

When I got home, I looked at the photos I took during the meal. They were terrible, so I couldn't share any of them!

2 Read the text again. Are the statements true (T) or false (F)?

1. Josie's granddad was angry when she started to use her phone. _____
2. Josie was surprised about her granddad's question. _____
3. Josie usually chooses the food she will eat at a restaurant before she gets there. _____
4. Josie's starter was better than her granddad's starter. _____
5. Josie's granddad chose a meat dish for the main course. _____
6. They didn't eat any desserts. _____
7. Josie's granddad will never use photos to choose food again. _____
8. Josie posted her photos of the meal online. _____

SPEAKING

1 Choose the correct form of the verbs to complete the suggestions and replies.

1
> Let's *going/go* to the Chinese restaurant on Saturday night.

2
> How about *having/have* some yoghurt for breakfast this morning?

3
> I don't feel like *eating/eat* a lot this evening.

4
> Shall we *asking/ask* Kay and Ron to join us for dinner?

5
> I don't mind *paying/pay* the higher prices because the restaurant is so good.

2 Complete the conversation with the words and phrases in the box.

| How about   I don't mind   I'm afraid   Let's |
| shall (x2)   That's a good idea |

Laura: What **1**............ we have for dinner tonight?
Marta: **2**............ making some pasta?
Laura: **3**............ I don't feel like having pasta tonight. **4**............ have a curry.
Marta: **5**............ . But what kind? We've got some chicken, or we could just use vegetables without any meat.
Laura: **6**............ .
Marta: OK, I think I'd prefer it with chicken.
Laura: Fine. **7**............ I start chopping the meat and vegetables, then?
Marta: Yes, if we both do it, it'll be quicker. I'm hungry!

WRITING

Complete the recipes with the words in the boxes. There is one word you do not need in each box.

A

| after   finally   first   then   until   when |

B

| finally   next   until   while |

EASY MUSHROOM SOUP

A **1**............ , wash and peel some mushrooms.
2............ chop them into very small pieces.
3............ that, peel an onion and cut it into very small pieces.
Put some butter in a pan and **4**............ it's hot, add the onion and mushrooms.
Cook the onion and mushrooms **5**............ they are soft.

B **6**............ the onion and mushrooms are cooking, boil some water.
Add the hot water and salt, pepper and some milk to the soft onion and mushrooms.
7............ , cook the onion and mushrooms in the water and milk for 20 minutes.
8............ , put the soup in a bowl and enjoy it with some fresh bread.

7 LIVE LIFE!

VOCABULARY

1 Write the hobby in the box for each person.

baking   doing exercise   doing Massaoke
doing photography   going to gigs
going to the gym   hanging out with friends
playing board games

1
I like making bread and cakes at home.

_____

2
My friends say the photos I take are really good.

_____

3
I joined one last month and I already feel quite fit.

_____

4
Doing nothing is great – we just sit and chat and drink lemonade!

_____

5
I enjoy games like chess.

_____

6
We get lots of good bands here and I love going to see them.

_____

7
I love singing with lots of other people.

_____

8
I hate sitting and doing nothing. Running and swimming are my favourite activities.

_____

2 Match the descriptions (1–5) with the words (a–e).

1 It isn't a large area, so the actors couldn't move around very much.

2 Everyone in the drama group is nervous because it's their last practice before the show.

3 The actor's wearing a large hat with a bright-yellow shirt, black trousers and dark-green boots.

4 There are still tickets available for the one on Thursday at 7.30.

5 There isn't one empty seat and everyone is enjoying watching the play.

a a performance
b a rehearsal
c a costume
d an audience
e the stage

3 Complete the sentences with the correct instruments.

1 You hold this long, straight instrument to your mouth to play it. _____ . (keyboard/violin/flute)

2 Pop and rock bands usually have one person playing the _____ . (drums/pianos/trumpets)

3 You put a _____ on your shoulder to play it. (drum/flute/violin)

4 You cannot carry a _____ . (keyboard/piano/drum)

5 A _____ is like a piano, but you have to switch it on! (flute/keyboard/violin)

6 Most _____ are made of metal. (violins/pianos/trumpets)

4 Complete the words for people in music with an ending in the box. Use some endings more than once. Then use the words to complete the description of Ed Sheeran.

-er   -ian   -ist   -r

1 songwrite _____
2 music _____
3 solo art _____
4 drumm _____
5 sing _____
6 guitar _____

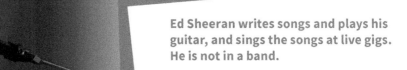

Ed Sheeran writes songs and plays his guitar, and sings the songs at live gigs. He is not in a band.

Ed is a _____ , a _____ , a _____ , a _____ and a _____ .

GRAMMAR

1 Read about brothers, Max and Joe. Complete the questions and short answers about them. Use the present perfect.

	MAX	JOE
win a game of chess	✓	✓
live near a desert	✗	✗
visit a country in Africa	✓	✓
speak to a famous person	✗	✓
go to a gig together	✗	✗

1 .... Joe ever .... a game of chess?
Yes, ...

2 .... Max and Joe ever .... near a desert?
.... , ...

3 .... Max and Joe ever .... a country in Africa?
.... , ...

4 .... Joe ever .... to a famous person?
.... , ...

5 .... Max and Joe ever .... to a gig together?
.... , ...

2 Complete the sentences about Joe and Max. Use *never* in the negative sentences.

1 Max .... a game of chess.
2 Max and Joe .... near a desert.
3 Max and Joe .... a country in Africa.
4 Max .... to a famous person.
5 Max and Joe .... to a gig together.

3 Write about what the people have just done. Use the correct form of the phrases in the box and *just*.

> drive into the garage   find it on the desk
> leave their flat   run up some stairs

1 Has Jim come home yet?
Yes. ....
2 Why is Samantha looking so hot and tired?
Because ....
3 Are you still looking for your key?
No. ....
4 Have Tom and Hannah arrived at the hotel yet?
No. .... !

1 11 Listen and choose one correct answer for each question.

1 Which club will Carla join?
 A History Club   **D** Running Club
 B Tennis Club   **E** Gym Club
 C Parkour Club

2 What will Johannes do in the club he has chosen?
 A try different jobs
 B help children in hospital
 C learn new board games
 D hang out with his student friends
 E help doctors

2 11 Listen again. Choose the correct answers to complete the sentences.

1 There are … clubs at the university.
 A 266   **B** 276   **C** 286

2 Johannes and Carla … think that clubs are important.
 A both
 B don't
 C possibly

3 Carla says she is not interested in clubs for
 A doing art.
 B social activities.
 C course subjects.

4 Johannes … parkour.
 A didn't enjoy
 B has never tried
 C doesn't understand

5 Johannes will go to the hospital
 A and start a club.
 B with other students.
 C to take some money.

6 Carla thinks Johannes' plan to work at the hospital will be
 A useful for the children.
 B useful for the doctors.
 C useful for Johannes.

For each question, choose the correct answer.

1

Lara – tonight my brother's taking me to my first ever gig so I can't go to drama club. See you at college tomorrow. Cathy

- **A** Cathy has never been to a gig before.
- **B** Cathy's brother will take her to college tomorrow.
- **C** Cathy doesn't want to go to drama club later.

2

BAKING FOR BEGINNERS
6-week course
Do advanced course afterwards for half the normal price

You pay less for your lessons if
- **A** you are a beginner.
- **B** you do a second course.
- **C** you pay for the whole six weeks.

3

CAN YOU PLAY AN INSTRUMENT?

Sandgate College music department is looking for musicians to teach weekly lessons to school children.

£20.00 per hour

The notice tells musicians
- **A** where the lessons will be.
- **B** how much money they will receive.
- **C** which instruments they will teach.

4

ART MUSEUM

Freda Medway will be here on Saturday, explaining how she made her latest painting.

This Saturday, at the art museum, you can
- **A** do some art.
- **B** learn about an artist's picture.
- **C** visit a new exhibition.

5

NOTICE

TEI RIVER
No fishing between 15 March and 15 June
More information at fishriver.com

- **A** There are two days when you cannot go fishing here.
- **B** If you want to catch fish here from March to June, get information online.
- **C** It is not possible to go fishing here any day in April or May.

6

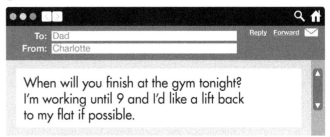

To: Dad
From: Charlotte

When will you finish at the gym tonight? I'm working until 9 and I'd like a lift back to my flat if possible.

What is Charlotte doing in her email?
- **A** asking her dad to take her home
- **B** telling her dad when she is going out
- **C** inviting her dad to do some exercise with her

PUSH YOURSELF B1

Choose the correct endings for the sentences.

1 I didn't hang out with my friends last night because
- **A** I had to study.
- **B** the rehearsal.

2 Marcia went for a run in the hot weather so
- **A** she needed some exercise.
- **B** she felt tired afterwards.

3 Eduardo phoned Sophia in the USA so that
- **A** he could tell her about his new job.
- **B** he had to pay a lot for his phone that month.

4 The students couldn't hear the teacher because of
- **A** he spoke very quietly.
- **B** the noise of traffic outside.

5 Pete burned the meat so
- **A** he was looking at something on his phone.
- **B** they just had vegetables for dinner.

6 Ollie won the game of chess because
- **A** a mistake Mike made.
- **B** he was a better player than Mike.

7 Carlotta stayed at home so that
- **A** she could watch her favourite series.
- **B** the jobs she needed to do.

8 Kristen stopped going to the gym because of
- **A** the cost.
- **B** it was too crowded.

SPEAKING

1 **Put the words in order to make answers to the questions.**

1 Why do you swim in the sea when the water's so cold?
it / makes / fantastic! / me / Because / feel

....

2 Why are you having flying lessons?
to / things. / new / think / it's / important / learn / I

....

3 Why do you do exercise every day?
after / to / me / relax / It / work. / busy / day / at / helps / a

....

4 What's the best thing about playing the drums?
a / rock / me / star! / feel / It / like / makes

....

5 What do you enjoy about your drama group?
think / be / stronger / I / helps / it / to / a / person. / me

....

2 **Match the questions (1–6) with the answers (a–f).**

1 What's your favourite free-time activity?
2 When do you have free time?
3 Who do you usually spend your free time with?
4 Tell me about a new activity you would like to try.
5 What was the best thing about last weekend?
6 Tell me about your plans for next weekend.

a I've always wanted to learn to play the guitar.
b I'm going to visit a friend who lives in Cadiz.
c My brother, Jose, or my best friend, Marco.
d Our football team won a match.
e Gaming. But I like playing football too.
f Some weekday evenings and Sundays. I have to help my dad in his shop on Saturdays.

WRITING

1 **Circle the negative or positive option in each sentence.**

1 If something is safe, it *is/isn't* dangerous.
2 If a musician is world-famous, a lot of people *know/don't know* him or her.
3 A delicious meal is one that *is/isn't* really nice.
4 Excellent *means/doesn't mean* the same as OK.
5 You describe a concert as special if there *is something/isn't anything* different about it.
6 Rap music *is/isn't* traditional.
7 If something is pleasant, it *is/isn't* nice.
8 Delicious *is/isn't* a word you usually use to describe buildings.
9 An amazing day is one that you *enjoyed/didn't enjoy* a lot.
10 An amazing day is one that *was/wasn't* surprising.

2 **Choose two correct words to complete each leaflet.**

| delicious | pleasant | special |

New burger restaurant!
Come and try the most ¹ ....
burgers in town!
² .... low prices for the first week!

| safe | traditional | world-famous |

Dance classes
Learn at the Bayford Dance School, now ³ ....
because of the many stars who began dancing here.
Lessons in ⁴ .... and modern dance. Classes for all ages.

| amazing | excellent | traditional |

Photographs of the city
New exhibition in the Art Museum

Catriona Deli has taken the most ⁵ .... photos,
showing the city as you've never seen it before.
Visit our café while you're here – serving ⁶ ....
coffee and snacks.

8 FEELS LIKE HOME

VOCABULARY

1 Write the words for types of homes in the sentences.

1. My aunt has a small ___ i l ___ a by the sea which we stay in during the summer.
2. I'd love to live in a small c ___ t ___ g ___ away from the city.
3. We live in a t ___ w ___ h ___ s ___ in a quiet street near the centre. It's got three floors.
4. I love being close to water, so it's great to live on a h ___ e b ___ t.
5. I live on my own and I don't need much space, so a s ___ u ___ i ___ l a ___ is perfect for me.
6. Our ___ p ___ r ___ m ___ t is on the first floor.

2 Complete the advertisement with the words in the box.

balcony	basement	building	furniture
garage	ground	neighbours	rent
roof	views		

BEAUTIFUL APARTMENT
NEAR PARK VADI IN ANKARA!

An apartment on the ¹ ___ floor of the apartment ² ___ .
Two bedrooms, sitting room, bathroom, kitchen and large ³ ___ outside the sitting room.
Kitchen table, chairs and some other ⁴ ___ included.
Garden on the ⁵ ___ at the top of the building, which you share with your ⁶ ___ – garden has beautiful ⁷ ___ of Park Vadi.
Large ⁸ ___ for cars in the ⁹ ___ under the apartments.
The ¹⁰ ___ is 3,300 Turkish Lira a month.

3 Look at the photo. Write the words next to each number.

1 ___   3 ___   5 ___
2 ___   4 ___   6 ___

4 Complete the definitions with the words in the box.

curtains	a lamp	a rug
a shelf	a sofa	stairs

1. This covers part of the floor and keeps our feet warm.
   ___
2. You walk up these to go to a higher floor in a building.
   ___
3. You put things like books on this.
   ___
4. These are at a window.
   ___
5. You can turn this on to help you read at night.
   ___
6. Two, three or more people can sit on this together.
   ___

GRAMMAR

1 Complete the sentences with the present perfect of the verbs in brackets and *yet* or *already*.

1 Josh is clean and ready to go out. He _____ (have a shower).

2 Jack and Victor are on the bus. They _____ (arrive at work).

3 The children are putting on their coats in the hall. They _____ (leave the house).

4 I'm not hungry. I _____ (eat).

5 Kim is answering the last few questions. She _____ (finish the exam).

6 We know Yves. We _____ (meet him).

7 Dylan doesn't need to get another T-shirt. He _____ (buy three).

8 They are still looking for a new flat. They _____ (find one they like).

2 Cross out the wrong phrases.

1 **since:** June   100 years   this morning
       three days   12 o'clock

2 **for:** 10 years   five minutes   half past 11
      Tuesday   a few hours

3 Complete the sentences using the present perfect or the past simple form of the verbs in brackets.

1 Chris _____ (finish) school in 2018. He _____ (not be) a school student since 2018.

2 Maria _____ (find) this flat five years ago. She _____ (rent) it for five years.

3 How long _____ you _____ (have) that fridge? We _____ (buy) it in 2010!

4 Where _____ Olivia _____ (go) last night? She _____ (not go) anywhere.

5 Priti and Anita _____ (know) Ivan and Dan since June. They _____ (meet) at a gig.

6 Nick _____ (be) my neighbour for 10 years. We _____ (live) in the same street since 2010.

1 Complete the sentences with the words and phrases in the box.

| forgotten | how to | it's called but | keep |
| kind of | part of | the English word | use it for |

1 I've _____ the word for this. It's a _____ long seat in the living room.

2 I don't know _____ say this. It's got a door and we _____ all kinds of things in it.

3 I don't know what _____ we _____ cooking food.

4 I don't know _____ for this. It's the _____ a house that is under the ground floor.

2 What do you think the things are in Exercise 1?

LISTENING PART 4

 12 For each question, choose the correct answer.

1 You will hear a woman talking about her home. What sort of home is it?
   A a townhouse
   B a city flat
   C a country cottage

2 You will hear a man talking to his wife about a sofa. What are they discussing?
   A what kind of sofa to get
   B where to put their new sofa
   C why they need another sofa

3 You will hear a woman talking to her friend about her flat. Why doesn't she want to live in it any more?
   A It's too expensive.
   B It isn't large enough.
   C It's not in the right area.

4 You will hear a man telling a friend about a problem in his apartment building. What is there a problem with?
   A the lift
   B the stairs
   C the garage

5 You will hear a woman telling her friend about her parents' new house. What does she like best about it?
   A the kitchen
   B the living room
   C the garden

READING

1 **Read and tick the topics that are in the text.**

A the type of home Giulia has ☐
B Giulia's plans for the future ☐
C a job Giulia had before ☐
D young farmers in Italy ☐
E how Giulia and Luca make money on the farm ☐
F the job Giulia and Luca have now ☐
G how Luca feels about life on the farm ☐

LIVING ON A FARM
BECOMES FASHIONABLE
IN ITALY!

1 Giulia Bianchi is an example of a change that is happening in Italy. She is a young farmer in the beautiful countryside of Tuscany, Italy. She lives in a pretty, traditional farmhouse with her husband and brother. They both work on the farm, too. But they haven't always been farmers.

2 Five years ago, Giulia and her husband, Luca, worked in a large bank in the city of Milan. They lived in a small, expensive studio apartment and worked long hours. They were not enjoying their lives. One weekend, they came to Tuscany to see Luca's parents. One of their neighbours had a small farm and he wanted to sell it. Giulia and Luca decided to buy it.

3 They left the city and started country life about four and a half years ago. They have worked really hard and now sell fruit and vegetables, and they also rent two of their old farm buildings as accommodation for tourists.

4 Giulia says, 'The buildings we rent are more comfortable than our house! We're always too busy to work on ours. We haven't painted any of the rooms since we came here! But I've lived in a small flat, so I know how great it is to have a bigger home.'

5 Living on a farm is getting more and more popular with young adults in Italy. In 2017, people under 30 started about 17% of new Italian farms – a lot more than in the past. People like Giulia believe that being a farmer is a better, more useful and more creative life than working all day every day in an office at a computer.

6 Giulia is very happy her life has changed. 'It's not an easy life, but it's never boring!' she says.

2 **Choose the correct description of each paragraph.**

Paragraph 1
A We learn about some problems that Italian farmers are having.
B We learn about a woman who lives in Tuscany, Italy.
C We learn about different kinds of homes in Italy.

Paragraph 2
A The writer explains how Giulia and Luca became farmers.
B The writer describes the good things about their city life.
C The writer tells us about Luca's parents selling their farm.

Paragraph 3
A The writer says how difficult it was to start their farm.
B The writer describes how they left the city.
C The writer explains what they do on the farm.

Paragraph 4
A Giulia tells us that she hated living in a small flat.
B Giulia talks about what she hasn't done yet in her home.
C Giulia says she needs to do more work on the tourist accommodation.

Paragraph 5
A The writer describes why young Italian people didn't like farming in the past.
B The writer tells us who most of the farmers are in Italy.
C The writer explains why more young people are starting farms in Italy.

Paragraph 6
A We learn how Giulia feels about living and working on the farm.
B We learn what Giulia does on the farm.
C We learn about a problem Giulia has on the farm.

SPEAKING

1 Complete the questions with the words in the box.

> anything   best   describe   home   part

1 What kind of _____ do you live in?
2 Which _____ of the country do you live in?
3 Is there _____ you don't like about your apartment?
4 What do you like _____ about the apartment?
5 Can you _____ your kitchen?

2 Choose the correct word to complete the sentences.

a I live on the *long/south/cheap* coast.
b It's a new apartment on the fourth *ground/flat/floor* of our building.
c There's a lot of traffic in my street, so it's *quiet/noisy/ expensive*.
d It's near some really nice *cafés/furniture/lifts* and shops.
e It's quite a small room, with white walls and grey *curtains/paintings/tiles* on the floor, and lots of shelves and cupboards.

3 Match the questions with the answers in Exercises 1 and 2.

1 _____   **4** _____
2 _____   **5** _____
3 _____

WRITING

1 Match the parts of the email phrases.

1 Dear   **a** soon
2 Best   **b** Rob
3 All   **c** things?
4 Hi   **d** the best
5 See you **e** Mrs Tyson
6 How are **f** wishes

2 Complete the email with the words and phrases in the box.

> All the best   at   Hello   How are you?
> I wanted to ask you   I'm writing to tell you
> My new apartment   near

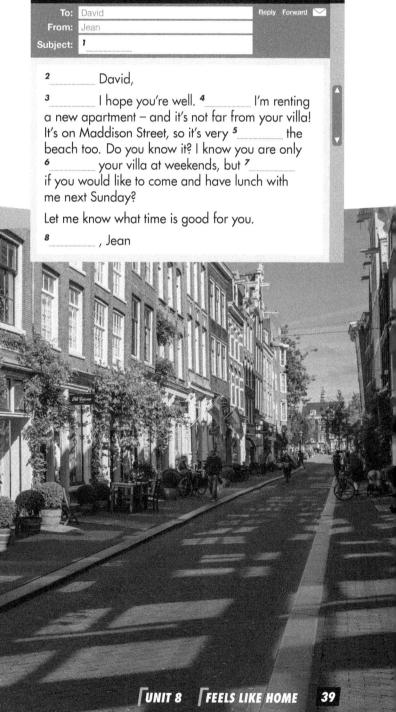

To: David   Reply Forward ✉
From: Jean
Subject: **1** _____

2 _____ David,

3 _____ I hope you're well. **4** _____ I'm renting a new apartment – and it's not far from your villa! It's on Maddison Street, so it's very **5** _____ the beach too. Do you know it? I know you are only **6** _____ your villa at weekends, but **7** _____ if you would like to come and have lunch with me next Sunday?

Let me know what time is good for you.

8 _____ , Jean

9 GETTING ALONG

VOCABULARY

1 Match the words (1–7) with the definitions (a–g).

1 A generous person is ....
2 A busy person is ....
3 A cool person is ....
4 A friendly person is ....
5 A reliable person is ....
6 A confident person is ....
7 A shy person is ....

a someone you can always believe.
b happy to give things to and do things for others.
c always doing something.
d not worried about meeting new people.
e easy to talk to and is always nice to other people.
f not comfortable when meeting new people.
g someone that people like because she/he looks great and does interesting things.

2 Complete the sentences with the words and phrases in the box.

angry   argue   bad mood   get on badly
get on well   good mood   worried

1 Henri feels great. The sun's shining and it's the beginning of his holiday. He's in a really ....
2 Kemal's dad has a bad back and his mum is working too hard. Kemal is .... about them.
3 Maria's brother has driven her car to college without asking first. She's .... with him.
4 Grace is feeling unhappy because she didn't pass her driving test. She's in a very ....
5 Martina and Georgia have been good friends for five years. They ....
6 Jessie and Rich agree about most things. They never .... about anything.
7 My two uncles are very different and don't agree about anything, so they ....

3 Complete the sentences with words for each section, A, B, C. There is one word you do not need in each section.

A | difficult   easy   exciting   happy |

1 Brendan's a very kind person so he's always .... to help his friends.
2 A lot of people enjoy travelling because it's .... to go to new places.
3 If you are a shy person, it is not .... to speak to a large audience.

B | agree   ask   decide   tell |

4 If you .... not to go to university, what will you do?
5 We didn't .... Karen to come to the party because she was on holiday.
6 When you spoke to Franz, did he .... to come to the meeting?

C | learn   prefer   teach   want |

7 I .... not to eat meat because I like animals.
8 Could you .... me to dance like you?
9 They don't .... to go shopping because it will be so busy today.

GRAMMAR

1 Complete each sentence with one word in each box. Put the verbs in the correct form.

| after   at   before   enjoy | eat   pay   play   ride |
| hate   start   without | watch   work   write |

1 William left his job in the hotel kitchen because he .... inside.
2 Jackson has a beautiful horse and he .... it every weekend.
3 You should always wash your hands .... a meal.
4 Lena was only four years old when she .... the violin.
5 Luis decided to go to Egypt .... a documentary about it.
6 Richa read a lot when she was young and now she's good .... stories.
7 Last night, I left the restaurant .... for my meal, so I need to go back there now!

2 **Read the conversation. Then complete the sentences with the *to* or *-ing* form of the verbs in brackets.**

Rashid: Shall we play tennis on Saturday afternoon?

Noel: I'm afraid I can't play in the afternoon.

Rashid: Oh, are you going into town?

Noel: No, I've got a guitar lesson with Mr Lemon. He's great. But I can play tennis before my lesson.

Rashid: OK. Let's book to play at the tennis club from 10 until 11.30. It's easy online. I'll meet you there.

Noel: Great!

Rashid: Don't forget your racket this time!

Noel: OK!

1 Rashid asked Noel .... tennis on Saturday. (play)

2 Rashid and Noel enjoy .... tennis together. (play)

3 Rashid wanted .... tennis in the afternoon. (play)

4 Noel is learning .... the guitar. (play)

5 Noel likes .... lessons with Mr Lemon. (have)

6 Rashid is happy .... to the tennis club in the morning. (go)

7 Noel and Rashid will finish .... tennis at 11.30. (play)

8 It isn't difficult .... tennis online. (book)

9 Rashid told Noel .... his racket. (not forget)

PUSH YOURSELF B1

Choose the correct option to complete the sentences.

1 I *am hoping/don't mind* swimming in a pool, but I prefer the sea.

2 I'm staying in bed a bit longer. I can't *be bothered/stand* to get up yet.

3 I *am planning/feel like* staying in tonight. I don't want to go out when it's so cold.

4 I'm not very *excited about/keen on* my holiday next month – we're going to such a boring place.

5 I've lost my car keys but I am *planning/hoping* to find them on my desk.

6 I haven't been shopping yet because I *can't be bothered/am planning* to go later this evening.

LISTENING PART 3

 13 For each question, choose the correct answer.

You will hear Laura talking to her friend Otto about Marla, the place where they live.

1 What kind of place is Marla?
  A an island
  B a small town
  C a village

2 What does Laura want to do in the city?
  A see a play
  B go shopping
  C go to the cinema

3 What does Otto like about Marla?
  A It is easy to find everything.
  B His street is pretty and quiet.
  C The people are friendly.

4 What does Otto enjoy doing in the mountains?
  A cycling
  B climbing
  C walking

5 What does Laura say about her brother?
  A Otto will like him.
  B Otto has already met him.
  C Otto can borrow his bike.

1 For each question, write the correct answer.

Write ONE word for each gap.

Example: **⁰** _would_

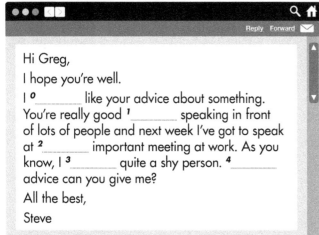

Hi Greg,

I hope you're well.

I **⁰** .... like your advice about something. You're really good **¹** .... speaking in front of lots of people and next week I've got to speak at **²** .... important meeting at work. As you know, I **³** .... quite a shy person. **⁴** .... advice can you give me?

All the best,

Steve

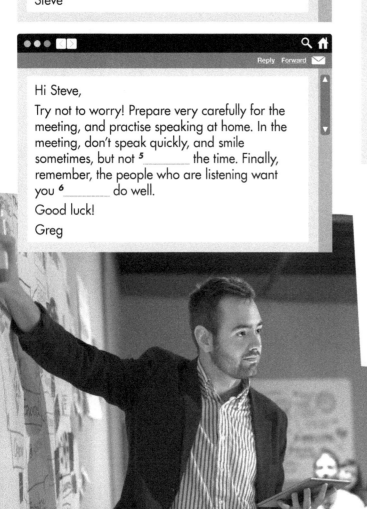

Hi Steve,

Try not to worry! Prepare very carefully for the meeting, and practise speaking at home. In the meeting, don't speak quickly, and smile sometimes, but not **⁵** .... the time. Finally, remember, the people who are listening want you **⁶** .... do well.

Good luck!

Greg

2 Read the email. Are the statements true (T) or false (F)? Correct the false statements.

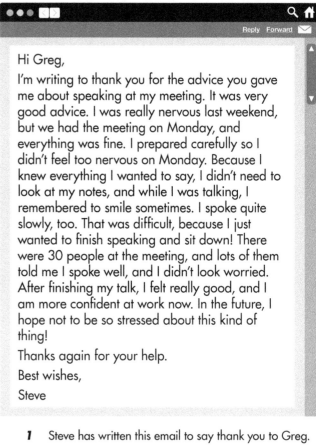

Hi Greg,

I'm writing to thank you for the advice you gave me about speaking at my meeting. It was very good advice. I was really nervous last weekend, but we had the meeting on Monday, and everything was fine. I prepared carefully so I didn't feel too nervous on Monday. Because I knew everything I wanted to say, I didn't need to look at my notes, and while I was talking, I remembered to smile sometimes. I spoke quite slowly, too. That was difficult, because I just wanted to finish speaking and sit down! There were 30 people at the meeting, and lots of them told me I spoke well, and I didn't look worried. After finishing my talk, I felt really good, and I am more confident at work now. In the future, I hope not to be so stressed about this kind of thing!

Thanks again for your help.

Best wishes,

Steve

1 Steve has written this email to say thank you to Greg.
....

2 Greg's advice didn't help Steve. ....

3 Steve felt less nervous on Monday than at the weekend. ....

4 Steve spoke at the meeting without using his notes.
....

5 It was easy for Steve to talk slowly. ....

6 Other people at the meeting thought Steve was worried. ....

7 Steve still feels shy at work. ....

SPEAKING

Complete the conversations with the correct expression for giving advice and the verbs in brackets.

1 A: Every time I go to the supermarket, I forget to buy some of the things I need!

   B: Why _____ a list? (write)

2 A: Do you know a fast way to get fit?

   B: No, I don't. You _____ the internet. (look on)

3 A: I'd like to spend less time on my phone, but it's really difficult.

   B: Try _____ for at least an hour every day. (turn off)

4 A: I find it impossible to get up early!

   B: You _____ bed so late! (go)

5 A: I never have enough time to cook a nice meal in the evening after work.

   B: What _____ some meals at the weekend? (prepare)

6 A: I live with a friend, and he listens to jazz music all the time. I hate it!

   B: Tell _____ some different sorts of music. (listen)

7 A: I forgot to wear my bike helmet twice last week.

   B: It isn't a good _____ without a helmet. (cycle)

WRITING

Complete the email with the phrases in the box.

best wishes could you tell me for your email
hear from you soon how about joining
I'd like to ask you it was great it's not expensive

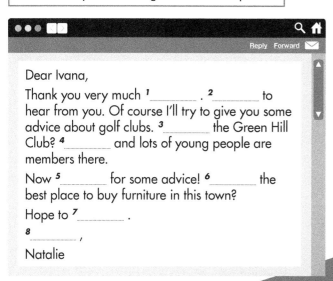

Dear Ivana,

Thank you very much **¹** _____ . **²** _____ to hear from you. Of course I'll try to give you some advice about golf clubs. **³** _____ the Green Hill Club? **⁴** _____ and lots of young people are members there.

Now **⁵** _____ for some advice! **⁶** _____ the best place to buy furniture in this town?

Hope to **⁷** _____ .

⁸ _____ ,

Natalie

10 OUT AND ABOUT

VOCABULARY

1 **Complete the sentences with the words in the box.**

> castle   department store   fountains
> library   stadium   statue   theatre

1 I usually sit by the .... in the park during my lunch break. I love the sound of the water.
2 I haven't got a guide book for my holiday so I'm going to borrow one from the ....
3 I saw a great play at the .... last night.
4 At the top of the hill, you can see the old stone walls of a .... that was there about 300 years ago.
5 Why don't you go to the .... in town? It sells everything you need for the kitchen and bedroom in your new flat.
6 To get to Beasley Street, turn left at the .... of the footballer.
7 We need to be at the .... at 3.15 so we'll have time to get to our seats before the match starts.

2 **Circle the positive or negative option in each sentence.**

1 Ships *go/don't go* on railway lines.
2 Different parts of a city *are/aren't* called districts.
3 Paths *are/aren't* for people to drive on.
4 Plants, people and animals *need/don't need* sunlight.
5 Gardens *are/aren't* indoor spaces.
6 You *should/shouldn't* go to a city centre to get fresh air.
7 You *can/can't* often sit on a bench in a park.

3 **Label the photos with the words in the box. There are two words you do not need.**

> bridge   bus stop   corner   crossing   roundabout
> square   traffic light   underground station

1 ....

2 ....

3 ....

4 ....

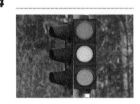

5 ....

6 ....

4 **Complete the conversations with the verbs in the box. For each conversation, there is one word you do not need.**

> excuse   get   know   turn   walk

A: ¹............... me. Do you ²............... where the Youth Theatre is?
B: Yes – ³............... straight down this street and ⁴............... right at the end.

> give   go   take   turn

A: Could you ⁵............... me directions to the university, please?
B: Of course. ⁶............... the first turning on the left into Hill Street, then ⁷............... straight on.

> be   get   see   tell

A: Can you ⁸............... me how to ⁹............... to the underground station, please?
B: Sure. Come out of the car park and you'll ¹⁰............... it on your right.

GRAMMAR

1 Complete the sentences with the words in the box.

may	may not	will	won't

1 It never rains at this time of year, so I .... take my raincoat.
2 Let's try this path – it .... go to the castle. I hope it does!
3 They've decided they .... buy the flat because it's too expensive.
4 He .... be here soon because he's just phoned from the end of the street!
5 We .... play the match tomorrow because I'm not sure if we have enough players.

might	might not	will	won't

6 We .... get a taxi to the station because we'd like to walk.
7 You .... see David at the gig because he didn't know if he could go.
8 I .... go shopping later. Do you want anything if I do?
9 This is not the right book so I .... take it back to the shop next time I go to town.
10 Do you like this dress? I .... buy it but I'm not sure about the colour.

2 Complete the conversation with *'ll* or *shall* and a verb in the box.

be	chop	drive	get	go
look	make	see	stay	

Tom: Come on. Let's start cooking dinner. Mum and Dad ¹ .... here in two hours.

Sara: OK. I ² .... up some vegetables for the soup.

Tom: ³ .... I .... a dessert?

Sara: Great idea – but what kind of dessert?

Tom: I don't know. I ⁴ .... in the fridge to see if we have any fruit.

Sara: OK.

Tom: Oh dear. There isn't any. ⁵ .... we .... shopping?

Sara: Why don't you go, and I ⁶ .... here. I can cook the soup and main course.

Tom: Right. I ⁷ .... there so I'm quicker.

Sara: Good idea.

Tom: ⁸ .... I .... some apples and then make apple cake?

Sara: Fantastic!

Tom: I'm going now. I ⁹ .... you in about half an hour.

Sara: Bye!

PUSH YOURSELF B1

Complete the sentences about city life with the words in the box.

historic	pavements	pedestrians	polluted
public transport	skyscraper	traffic jams	traffic-free

SOME GOOD THINGS ABOUT CITY LIFE	SOME BAD THINGS ABOUT CITY LIFE
¹ .... is usually better than in towns or villages so you don't need a car.	The air is ⁵ .... because there is so much traffic.
You can go to the top of a ² .... and see an amazing view of the city.	Walking along the ⁶ .... is difficult because they're so busy.
In old cities, there are interesting ³ .... places to visit.	It may be dangerous for ⁷ .... to cross the streets.
You can enjoy shopping and being a tourist, especially in areas that are ⁴	It takes a long time to drive anywhere when there are ⁸ ....

LISTENING PART 2

 14 For each question, write the correct answer in the gap. Write one word or a number or a date or a time.

You will hear an advertisement for a new department store.

New Department Store

New:	Richards Department Store!
Address:	Victoria *Square*
Next to:	¹ a ....
Date it opens:	² .... June
Daily closing time:	³ .... p.m.
Places to eat on:	⁴ .... floor
Free gift in first week:	⁵ ....

1 Read the text and tick the things it mentions.

A which years past Olympic Games happened in	☐
B where the next summer Olympic Games will be	☐
C some of the cities that have had the summer Olympic Games	☐
D what some Olympic buildings have become	☐
E what the Olympic Games is	☐
F which cities have not used any Olympic buildings again after the games finished	☐

AFTER THE OLYMPICS

The Olympic Games is an international sports competition that happens every four years. It is in a different city every year. It's very expensive to hold the Olympics because the cities have to build new stadiums, villages for the sports people and lots more. **1** _____ However, some cities have found great ways to use the places they built for the Olympics.

In 2008, the summer Games were in Beijing, China, and the swimming and diving competitions took place in a beautiful new building called the Water Cube. **2** _____ Beijing families and tourists from all over the world go to have fun there. When you enter the Water Cube, you feel like you are going under the sea.

The 1980 Summer Olympics were in Moscow, Russia. The Russians used a lot of buildings that were already there, so they didn't need to build as many new buildings as other Olympic cities. **3** _____ Most of these are still homes today, and people are still using the Olympic horse-riding centre and the big Olympic sports stadium.

In summer 1992, the Olympic Games came to Barcelona, Spain. **4** _____ This is because for the Olympics, the city improved lots of its spaces. One example is four kilometres of new beaches beside the city. These changes have helped it become one of the favourite cities for people to visit in Europe today.

The Summer Olympics of 2012 took place in London, England. **5** _____ London spent a lot of money on these parts of the city. They improved homes, parks and public transport for people to use during and after the Olympics. Also, the Olympic stadium is now a football stadium for the London club West Ham.

2 Choose the correct sentences to complete the text. There is one sentence you do not need.

A The Olympic stadiums were in some of the poorer districts in the east of the city.

B This has now become the country's largest water park.

C After the Olympics, it is difficult to use some of the buildings.

D The city planned these changes very carefully for several years before the Games.

E Many people think that the city is more popular with tourists because of the Olympics.

F But of course they had to build a new sports stadium and some apartments.

SPEAKING

Choose the two best answers for each question.

1 Where is your town?
  A I live in the centre.
  B It's in the south west of the country.
  C It's quite near Alicante.

2 Please tell me something about the street where you live.
  A I live in a flat with my brother.
  B There are lots of trees and it's quiet.
  C It has lots of new houses and a few shops.

3 How often do you go to the theatre in your town?
  A about once a month
  B I walk or take the tram.
  C Never! I don't enjoy it.

4 What do you think is the most beautiful building in your town?
  A The new library is really lovely.
  B The old castle is fantastic.
  C I'd like a new sports centre.

5 Where is the best place to eat in your town?
  A Most people eat a lot of fish and pasta.
  B At a fantastic restaurant by the river called Victor's.
  C The main square – there are lots of good places.

6 How do people travel around in your town?
  A There are no trains, so most people ride bikes or walk.
  B Well, lots of people drive their cars because there aren't enough buses.
  C It's slow when there's a lot of traffic after work in the evening.

7 What do you like doing at weekends in your town?
  A I prefer my weekends to my work days.
  B I enjoy cycling in the hills.
  C Hanging out with friends in one of the coffee shops.

WRITING

Write the sentences to complete the email.

a forget / the / of / city. / I'll / never / fantastic / that / view / seeing

....

b meet / was / It / to / him. / great

....

c day. / a / had / wonderful / I

....

d amazing / ever / most / the / I've / market / been to. / It's

....

e moment / we / favourite / was / the / top. / when / at / arrived / My

....

f city. / looking / I'm / to / the / showing / you / forward

....

> Hi Esin,
>
> I'm writing to thank you for showing me around Bursa yesterday. **¹**...............
> I loved visiting the Great Mosque and the covered market. **²**............... I also really enjoyed going up the mountain, Uludağ. **³**............... It was amazing.
> **⁴**............... I hope you can come to visit me in Ankara soon. **⁵**...............
> Say hello to your brother from me. **⁶**...............
> Love from,
> Katie

11 SAVING AND SPENDING

VOCABULARY

1 Complete the sentences with the words in the box.

> bill   discounts   receipt
> reduced items   salary   sale

1 You can save a lot of money in a supermarket by buying _____ .
2 You usually get a _____ after you've paid for something in a shop.
3 Shops often have a _____ at the end of a season.
4 A _____ tells you how much you will have to pay for a service like car repairs.
5 A doctor's _____ is usually more than a shop assistant's.
6 Students often get _____ on tickets for transport, concerts and the cinema.

2 Choose the correct verbs to complete the sentences.

1 I didn't have enough money for the dress so I *lent/ borrowed/saved* some from my brother.
2 Strawberries *spend/cost/pay* more in the winter than in the summer here.
3 I've *cost/saved/wasted* enough money to get the leather jacket I want. I'm going shopping!
4 I *paid/saved/spent* all my money when I went shopping, so I can't go out tonight.
5 Jack wants to be a famous footballer so he can *earn/ pay/lend* a lot of money.
6 I *cost/borrowed/wasted* a lot of money on my theatre tickets – I was ill so I couldn't go.
7 My dad *spent/paid/lent* the bill for the meal. It was really kind of him.
8 The bank *earned/borrowed/lent* my mum some money to buy a car.

3 Match the beginnings (1–7) with the endings (a–g) of the questions.

1	*Customer:*	Excuse me, are you the _____
2	*Customer:*	Have you got this T-shirt in a larger _____
3	*Shop assistant:*	Would you like to try _____
4	*Customer:*	I want to see if this dress is long enough. Where's the _____
5	*Customer:*	I'd like to pay for this now. Where's the _____
6	*Shop assistant:*	Would you like to pay _____
7	*Customer:*	This cost £8.50 and I gave you £10, so can I have my _____

a in cash or by card?   **e** those jeans on?
b shop assistant?   **f** size?
c changing room?   **g** till?
d change?

GRAMMAR

1 Complete the sentences about schedules with the correct form of the verbs in the box.

> arrive   close   leave   start

1 The bus for the study trip _____ at 8.30 am. Don't be late!
2 What time _____ the Golden Beach restaurant _____ ? At 11.30 pm.
3 The college show _____ at 7.30 pm.
4 What time _____ the flights from Milan _____ in London? At 15.00 and 19.00.

2 Complete the sentences with the present continuous or present simple form of the verbs in brackets.

1 William and Martin _____ (take) their grandma to the theatre on Saturday.
2 Roberta _____ (not go) out with her friends this afternoon. She's busy.
3 I _____ (work) in my uncle's shop every day next week.
4 How many stations _____ that train _____ (stop) at?
5 Which friend _____ you _____ (meet) for dinner next weekend?
6 Both the films that we want to see _____ (start) at the same time. That's a shame.

3 Complete the sentences with *going to* or the present continuous and the verbs in brackets.

1 **A:** Are you ¹_____ (do) anything this weekend?

B: Yes, I'm very excited. My brother ²_____ (get married) on Saturday. How about you?

A: Our volleyball team ³_____ (play) in a tournament this weekend. The first game begins at 9.00, so we ⁴_____ (stay) in a hotel the night before.

2 **A:** Guess what! I've just won £5,000 in a competition!

B: What ⁵_____ (you/spend) it on?

A: I ⁶_____ (save) it and then when I have enough money I ⁷_____ (buy) a car.

READING

1 Read the article. What is Francis writing about? Choose the TWO best answers.

A giving advice to people about keeping food

B explaining why he wanted to change his shopping habits

C describing how he has saved money on food

D telling everyone that they must stop wasting food

WASTING FOOD, WASTING MONEY
By Francis Vernon

Two months ago, I went to the supermarket and bought lots of food, including some tomatoes and some strawberries. I got two boxes of strawberries for the price of one, and I bought a large box of tomatoes because they were reduced. When I got home, I opened my fridge and I found I already had some strawberries and some tomatoes. After a few days, I still had one packet of strawberries and some tomatoes but I couldn't use them because they were black and soft.

When I saw this, I was angry with myself. 'This is not clever!' I thought, and decided I must stop wasting money on things I will never use. I read some blogs to get some ideas on how to do this and changed how I shop for food.

I've learned that the best way to stop wasting food is to shop more often. That sounds strange, but it's better because I don't buy a lot each time. This means the fridge is never full, so it's easy to remember exactly what I've got. Also, I don't buy food to eat several days in the future, when I may not want to eat it for various reasons. Another thing I do is to make sure I eat all the oldest things first.

When I'm planning a meal, instead of looking in a recipe book and then looking in the fridge, I start by looking in the fridge, see what's there, and then I decide what to make with it.

I feel much happier about the way I spend money these days. I spend less, and I put less in the bin. It's better for me and better for the world!

Complete the text with the words and phrases in the box.

afford	bank account	bargains	on credit
owes	second-hand	value for money	worth

Valentina is a student and she lives at home with her parents. She has a ¹_____ but it is usually empty! She earns money in a café at weekends, but sometimes it isn't enough. If she wants to buy something she can't ²_____, she sometimes borrows money from her mum. At the moment, she ³_____ her mum €50. She borrows from her mum because she doesn't want to buy anything ⁴_____ with a bank card. She never buys ⁵_____ things because she likes to have everything new, but she loves shopping for ⁶_____ in clothes shops. She loves it when she pays only a little for something that is ⁷_____ a lot of money. If she sees something that is good ⁸_____, she feels like she just has to buy it!

2 Read the article again. Complete the sentences with one, two or three words from the text.

1 At the supermarket, Francis bought some _____ for half their normal price.

2 In his fridge at home, Francis had some _____ and some _____ before he went to the supermarket.

3 When he wasted some food, Francis felt _____ and decided he must not do it again.

4 Francis got some advice from _____ about how to stop wasting food.

5 Francis now goes shopping _____ than before.

6 Now, when Francis is deciding what to cook, he looks _____ first.

7 Francis is happy because he is saving money and also helping the _____.

LISTENING PART 1

  15 For each question, choose the correct answer.

1 Where is Anna going next week?

2 What is Alejandro going to buy?

A **B** **C**

3 In which month does Antonio's English course start?

4 What time does the shop close?

5 What kind of music will there be at tonight's concert?

SPEAKING

1 Complete the sentences with one word or phrase in each box. Sometimes both *as* and *because* are possible.

as	because	so	That's why

delicious	lovely little	old and dirty	really boring

1
Yes, I bought a new phone case yesterday _____ the one I had before was very _____ .

2
I enjoy buying bike equipment _____ I love bikes and cycling. I hate shopping for clothes. I think that's _____ .

3
I got it in a _____ shop in my town. A lot of shops are closing in my town. _____ I went there instead of buying it on the internet.

4
A chocolate shop in the city is the best shop I know. It's a wonderful place, with hundreds of different kinds of _____ chocolate, _____ I always spend a long time choosing the ones I want.

2 Match the questions (a–d) with the answers (1–4) in Exercise 1.

a Where did you buy that belt?
b What's your favourite shop?
c Have you bought anything recently?
d What sort of things do you like buying?

WRITING

Complete the review of a bookshop with the words in the box.

All in all	Another good	Another negative
bargains	building	go back	high point	near
One bad	One of the best	the worst thing
wouldn't recommend		

I went to the Hillstreet Bookshop last weekend. It's a very large bookshop **1**_____ the train station. It's in an old **2**_____ which has three floors. **3**_____ things about it is that it has so many books in different languages. **4**_____ thing is the seats. You can choose a book and sit and read it. But the **5**_____ for me was the brilliant sale on the ground floor! I got some great **6**_____ there.

Not everything was good, however. **7**_____ thing was that there was no lift, so some people can't go up to the top floor. **8**_____ point for me was the way the shop looked – the colours were all dark and some of the shelves needed repairs. But **9**_____ for me was the shop assistants. They didn't know anything about the books and didn't want to help me.

10_____ , it's an OK shop for some kinds of books, but I **11**_____ it and I'm not going to **12**_____ there.

VOCABULARY

1 Complete the crossword with the school subjects.

			¹	O			²G			
			³							
			H							⁴
		⁵	S		⁶	A				S
		R								T
						H				
⁷	H		M	S						
										Y

2 Tick the correct boxes with the number of ticks shown. In which subjects are you most likely to ... ?

	HISTORY	GEOGRAPHY	MATHS	DRAMA	PHYSICS	MODERN LANGUAGES
1 ... find out about people in different countries? ✓✓✓	✓	✓				✓
2 ... do equations? ✓✓						
3 ... find out about the Earth? ✓✓						
4 ... do experiments? ✓						
5 ... take part in performances? ✓						
6 ... write essays? ✓✓						
7 ... do research? ✓✓✓						

3 Answer the questions with the words and phrases in the box.

a degree   get good marks   graduate
primary school   a qualification   secondary school

1 Where do teenagers go to learn? ....

2 What do you get when you finish a course at school, college or university? ....

3 What do you do when you finish university? ....

4 What do students hope to do after they write an essay? ....

5 What do you get when you complete a university course? ....

6 Which is the first school that children go to? ....

4 Complete the conversation with the correct form of the verbs in the box.

fail   pass   revise   study   take

Katya: Rosie, which exams have you got in June?

Rosie: History and French.

Katya: ¹ .... you .... for them now?

Rosie: Not yet. I'm going to start ² .... for them next week.

Katya: Do you think you will ³ .... them?

Rosie: I hope so! If I ⁴ .... them, I'll have to ⁵ .... them again in September.

5 Complete the text with the words and phrases in the box.

boss   break   day off
diploma   long hours   staff

I'm a student on a business ¹ .... course and at weekends I'm a shop assistant in a department store. I really like the job. It's easy work and I don't work ² .... , just 10–4 on Saturday and Sunday, with a ³ .... for lunch. My ⁴ .... is nice, too. She's the manager of our part of the store, and she tells me what to do really clearly and helps me if I have any questions. If I need to take a ⁵ .... , it's usually not a problem if I tell her at least a week before. The other ⁶ .... who work with me are friendly and we have lots of fun at work.

GRAMMAR

1 **Put the words in order to make sentences.**

1 ill. / eat / If / I / fish / feel / I

....

2 if / don't / Plants / they / water. / have / die

....

3 too / hot / close / The / room / you / if / the / windows. / is

....

4 you / Phones / if / drop / them. / sometimes / break

....

5 we / If / to / Rome / visit / we / my family / there. / go / can

....

6 get / you / very dirty / if / them. / don't clean / Cars

....

2 **Match the two parts of the first conditional sentences (1–6) and (a–f). Then complete the sentences with the correct form of the verbs in brackets.**

1 If the train arrives late at the airport, ...

2 You won't have enough money for the video game

....

3 If you have any questions during the tour,

....

4 If the mangoes in the supermarket are very small,

....

5 We'll go to the cinema ....

6 Bernardo will win the whole competition

....

a if it .... (rain) on holiday

b the guide .... (try) to answer them

c if he .... (win) another game

d I .... (not buy) any

e we .... (miss) our flight

f if I .... (not lend) you some

3 **Complete the passive sentences. Use *by* if necessary.**

1 Someone built the house 100 years ago.
The house .... 100 years ago.

2 Someone makes the shoes in Italy.
The shoes .... in Italy.

3 Someone told the students to go home early.
The students .... to go home early.

4 Everyone enjoyed the party.
The party .... everyone.

5 Thousands of people visit the museum each month.
The museum .... thousands of people each month.

6 People take the exams every December.
The exams .... every December.

LISTENING PART 4

16 For each question, choose the correct answer.

1 You will hear a woman asking her friend James about college.
What did James do this morning?
A write an essay
B do some research
C take an exam

2 You will hear a woman talking about school.
What was her favourite subject at school?
A drama
B art
C music

3 You will hear a man talking to a friend about an exam.
Why did their friend Tom fail the exam?
A He didn't study enough.
B He didn't complete the exam.
C He didn't feel well.

4 You will hear a girl talking to her dad about university.
What does the girl's dad suggest that she does?
A study physics
B find a place to study
C speak to her maths teacher

5 You will hear a woman talking to a friend about her job.
Why does she like her job?
A She makes a lot of money.
B She has a nice boss.
C She has learned a lot.

Complete the sentences with *if, when* or *unless*.

1 Henry will fail the exam _____ he revises more this week.
2 _____ winter comes, we'll go skiing.
3 You can't be an engineer _____ you have the right qualifications.
4 I'll ask Jim to play tennis _____ Katherine can't.
5 _____ the traffic's really bad in Fleet Street, the bus will be here soon.
6 _____ I get good marks in this essay, I'll pass my course.
7 _____ we arrive at the theatre, we have to get our tickets from the ticket office.

READING

1 Read the text. Choose the best title for it.

A How school changed me
B How I learned from my mistakes
C How I became interested in my subject

2 Read the text again. Match the beginnings (1–6) with endings (a–i) of the sentences about the text. There are three answers you do not need.

1 Eduardo enjoyed doing art at _____
2 Eduardo became interested in science when he was a student at _____
3 Becky learned about a pilot when she was at _____
4 Becky began building model planes because of a visit to _____
5 Joshua was told about yoghurt by his _____
6 Joshua did some experiments with his _____

a teacher.
b mother.
c a toy shop.
d primary school.
e home.

f equipment.
g secondary school.
h a museum.
i sister.

EDUARDO
CHEMISTRY STUDENT

When I was a primary school student, I wanted to be an artist. I loved spending my free time painting and making things with my sister at our kitchen table. Later, at secondary school, I became really interested in photography and cameras. I had a great teacher, and she taught us how to use all the cameras and photography equipment the school had. Instead of using modern digital cameras, we used old ones, so we had to make photos from film. That was when I learned how amazing chemistry was, and I began to love science.

BECKY
ENGINEERING STUDENT

After a teacher at my primary school read us a story about a famous pilot, I asked my mum to take me to an aeroplane museum. I found out a lot about the history of flying there. Then, when I was 13, I was taken to a large toy shop which sold all the equipment you need to make model planes. That was when I started making them. After building each model, I painted it and put it on my bookshelf. Then I read all about that plane and the people who flew it.

JOSHUA
BIOLOGY STUDENT

When I was about eight, one of my primary school teachers said that yoghurt was made from milk. So I asked my mum to buy some milk because I wanted to do an experiment with it. My sister and I put some in a bowl and took it outside, then left it in the sun. After a few days it looked like yoghurt. We tried a little bit of it. It was terrible! But after that, we did all kinds of other experiments with food and plants and we both became more and more interested in science.

SPEAKING

1 Read the questions. Tick which person asks the question at an interview.

		INTERVIEWER	PERSON APPLYING FOR JOB
0	So, you're 19 years old, is that right?	✓	
1	Will I get a lunch break?		
2	Can you tell us about your qualifications and experience?		
3	How much time off will I get each week?		
4	What salary are you offering?		
5	Is the uniform provided?		
6	Can you tell us about your other skills?		
7	Am I going to work in a team?		
8	Have you worked in a factory before?		
9	Who will be my boss?		
10	How many hours will I work?		

2 Match the answers (a–j) with the questions (1–10) above.

a In your first year, you will get £24,000.
b I speak Japanese and I can drive a car.
c Yes. You'll work with five other members of staff.
d Yes, but you will need to wear your own black shoes.
e You will do 40 a week.
f No, but I learn new things very quickly!
g It will be the General Manager, Henrik Lars.
h Yes. You'll get 45 minutes each day.
i I've got a diploma in IT and I've worked for six months in a shop.
j You won't have to work at weekends.

WRITING

Write the sentences in a job application email using the words given. Put the verbs in the correct form.

Dear Miss Davis,

1 I / write / apply / for the job of waiter / as / advertise / in your café.

2 I / attach / CV / with my qualifications and experience.

3 As you / see from my CV / I / have / work in another café for a year / and / have / a diploma in business studies.

4 I / be / always / very friendly and polite.

5 I / look forward / hear from you.

Yours sincerely,
Martina Barr

Silver Coast Café
WAITER WANTED

Must have experience
Must be friendly and polite
Apply by email with CV to
gdavis@silvercoast.net

VOCABULARY

1 Match the beginnings of the sentences (1–5) with the endings (a–e).

1 My best friend has three sisters but ....
2 My Aunt Harriet lives near us but ....
3 I have a girlfriend now but ....
4 My fiancé is called Vince and ....
5 We had a family party on Saturday because ....

a I was single for a year before I met her.
b all my other relatives live in other cities.
c I'm an only child.
d my parents have been married for 25 years.
e we've been engaged for six months.

2 Choose the correct options to complete the sentences.

1 Stephen Hawking was one of the most *annoying/brilliant/confident* scientists of the twentieth century.
2 Shy people are not *kind/sweet/confident* with others.
3 Flying insects are very *annoying/lazy/sociable* if they get into your bedroom at night.
4 Babies look very *lazy/kind/sweet* when they are sleeping.
5 It is surprising when a *sociable/quiet/brilliant* person suddenly talks a lot.
6 *Sweet/Annoying/Sociable* people usually love parties and meeting new people.
7 If you live with a *confident/quiet/lazy* person, you might have to do most of the cleaning and cooking.
8 Primary school teachers need to be *kind/quiet/confident* to the children in their classes.

3 Complete the sentences with the words in the box.

casual cool fashionable smart sporty

1 Someone who often wears trainers, football shorts and a football shirt is ....
2 Someone who wants to look good all the time, and perhaps wears sunglasses a lot, is ....
3 Someone who reads magazines and looks online for the newest ideas and the best new brands is ....
4 Someone who is having an interview usually needs to wear .... clothes.
5 Someone who doesn't like suits or very fashionable clothes usually wears .... clothes.

4 Write the words in the box under the correct photo.

handbag jewellery sandals suits sunglasses tie trainers

....

....

....

....

....

....

....

GRAMMAR

1 Complete the questions with the correct form of *be like* or *look like*.

1 **A:** My sister's fiancé is called Paul.
 B: What ....?
 A: He's tall and slim, with short blond hair.

2 **A:** I met my cousin Beatrice for the first time yesterday!
 B: Great! What ....?
 A: She's really funny, friendly and smiles all the time.

3 **A:** Ben and Frederica are my best friends.
 B: What ....?
 A: They're both quite confident, and very kind.

4 **A:** Do you know Cara Maxwell?
 B: What ....?
 A: She's got long, straight, red hair and she's quite short.

2 Complete the sentences with an adjective in the box in the comparative form.

bad	boring	good looking
happy	short	thin

1 Nick is taller than Steve. Steve is .... Nick.

2 My white cat is fatter than my black cat. My black cat is .... my white cat.

3 I think my brothers are worse looking than me! I think I am .... my brothers!

4 Today, I'm sadder than I was yesterday. Yesterday, I was .... I am today.

5 My dad's cooking is better than my mum's. My mum's cooking is .... my dad's.

6 Watching football is more interesting than watching golf. Watching golf is .... watching football.

3 Complete the sentences with superlative adjectives.

1 June is hotter than any other month. June is .... month.

2 The car park is uglier than any other building in town. The car park is .... building in town.

3 Your baby's sweeter than any baby I've ever seen. Your baby is .... baby I've ever seen.

4 I think no subject is more interesting than maths. I think maths is .... subject.

5 The fish dishes are more expensive than anything else on the menu. The fish dishes are .... dishes on the menu.

6 Nobody in the team is a better player than Harry. Harry is .... player in the team.

7 I have never seen a worse film. It's .... film I have ever seen.

LISTENING PART 3

 17 For each question, choose the correct answer. You will hear Jo talking to her mum about her mum's Grandpa Bill.

1 Where did Jo find the old book?
 A in a box
 B on some shelves
 C in a cupboard

2 What kind of person was Grandpa Bill?
 A sociable
 B quiet
 C funny

3 What did Jo's mum like doing with Grandpa Bill?
 A baking bread
 B riding his horse
 C reading books

4 What was Grandpa Bill's job?
 A He was a teacher.
 B He was a factory worker.
 C He was a doctor.

5 Where did Grandpa Bill meet Grandma Annie?
 A at the cinema
 B in the town hall
 C at the theatre

Complete the second sentence so it means the same as the first sentence. Use *as ... as* or *not as ... as*.

1 Jim and Ned are both clever.
Ned _____ Jim.

2 Black Mountain and Goat Mountain are both high.
Goat Mountain _____ Black Mountain.

3 June was warmer than May.
May _____ June.

4 The book is better than the film.
The film _____ the book.

5 Flying is often more expensive than going by train.
Going by train _____ flying.

6 For me, maths is easier than chemistry.
For me, chemistry _____ maths.

READING

Read the text. Match the descriptions (1–6) with the correct paragraph (A–F).

1 The writer explains that feeling happy or sad makes us choose different colours.

2 The writer explains why people do not like wearing some colours.

3 The writer asks questions about the reasons for people doing something.

4 The writer gives you an idea for something to try.

5 The writer explains that a person's personality affects the colours they choose to wear.

6 The writer explains that we wear different colours in different seasons.

CHOOSING THE COLOURS OF OUR CLOTHES

A When you go to your wardrobe and choose some black jeans and a green T-shirt to wear, do you know why? Why didn't you want to wear the red T-shirt and white jeans?

B One answer to these questions is that we choose certain types of colour at different times of year. In countries with a hot summer and a cold winter, the colours we wear in spring and summer are usually lighter and brighter than autumn and winter clothes.

C One other reason we choose the colours we wear is our mood that day. If we're in a bad mood, we don't usually put on bright pink, white or yellow clothes for example. But we might wear these colours if we're in a really good mood. If our mood changes during the day, clothes we choose in the morning stop feeling comfortable, and we may want to change them.

D There may also be a colour that you never wear because you hate it. This may be because you've had a bad experience while you were wearing that colour or it may be because you think that the colour will tell people something negative about you. For example, some men don't wear pink because they think it's a colour that only women should wear.

E Another reason for hating a colour is that it does not match the type of person that you are. For example, if you're a quiet, shy person, you probably don't like wearing orange, but you might wear it a lot if you are a confident, sociable person.

F So next time you go to your wardrobe, think about why you are choosing those colours. And why not do an experiment? Wear a different colour and see how you feel in it.

SPEAKING

Complete the conversation with the words and phrases in the box.

could be	don't think	looks	Maybe	Perhaps
probably	're wearing	sure	think	've got

Patricia: Look at this photo of me and you when we were children!

Paula: Oh yes! We ¹_____ those pink dresses that Mum made for us!

Patricia: And we ²_____ really long hair! Where are we?

Paula: I ³_____ we're on holiday. I'm ⁴_____ that's not our old house.

Patricia: You're right. ⁵_____ we're at Grandma's house.

Paula: Yes, we ⁶_____ are. But who's that woman in the photo? It's not Grandma.

Patricia: I'm not sure. But I ⁷_____ she's happy. She ⁸_____ quite angry!

Paula: ⁹_____ she doesn't like children!

Patricia: She ¹⁰_____ Grandma's neighbour, Rosa. Do you remember her?

Paula: Oh yes!

WRITING

1 **Read the paragraphs of a product review. Put them in the correct order. Write the paragraph letter (A–D) in the table.**

PARAGRAPH 1:	Introduction	....
PARAGRAPH 2:	The good things about the product	....
PARAGRAPH 3:	The bad things about the product	....
PARAGRAPH 4:	Conclusion: overall opinion of the product and recommendation	....

A ¹_____ , it was quite heavy to carry. So it is not a good one to get if you are planning to walk a long way with it. There are also lots of cheaper tents of the same size available if you look online.

B ²_____ Well, ³_____ . If you need a tent for a walking holiday, ⁴_____ . But if you want a cool tent that will really keep you dry, even in heavy rain, then this is one of the best.

C I bought my *Nature's Home* tent from the outdoors activity store in my town last month. I bought it to take to a music festival, and I'm very glad I did!

D ⁵_____ the tent's fantastic design as soon as I saw it in the store. ⁶_____ I've ever seen, and because it's pink and yellow, it was really easy to find amongst hundreds of other tents at the festival camping site. ⁷_____ about the tent is that it kept me dry! It rained one night at the festival, but nothing inside my lovely new tent got wet.

2 **Complete the paragraphs in Exercise 1 with the phrases in the box.**

But for me, the best thing	I fell in love with
it depends on what you want.	It's the coolest tent
On the less positive side	So do I recommend the tent?
then it is not a good buy	

14 PLAY IT, WATCH IT, LOVE IT

VOCABULARY

1 **Which sport are these things used for? Label the photos with the words in the box.**

athletics   basketball   cricket
football   rugby   tennis

1 _____   2 _____

3 _____   4 _____

5 _____   6 _____

2 **Are these statements true (T) or false (F)?**

1 When you play cricket, you try to score goals.
   _____

2 Basketball players can't pick up the ball and throw it during a game. _____

3 In a tennis match, you try to win points. _____

4 Rugby is a game between two teams of five people.
   _____

5 There are many different kinds of races in football.
   _____

6 Players try to hit a ball with a bat in cricket. _____

7 There is usually a net on a football goal. _____

8 Basketball players use a racket. _____

3 **Complete the sentences with the words and phrases in the box.**

lose   pitch   red card   referee   rules   sent off

1 In football, there is a goal at each end of the _____ .

2 Football fans often think the _____ is wrong.

3 If a player is shown a _____ , they have to leave the match.

4 When a player is _____ , his or her team has to play with 10 players.

5 Players have to learn the _____ of the game.

6 Players don't want to _____ a match.

4 **Match the questions (1–7) with the answers (a–g).**

1 What might you get when you come first in a race?
   _____

2 Who is a person who has won something? _____

3 Who is a person who has won lots of races or matches?
   _____

4 In what do you have to run 3,000 metres or more?
   _____

5 Who does a sport as a job? _____

6 What must sports people do to improve? _____

7 In what do you try to win something? _____

a   a long-distance race
b   a winner
c   train
d   a competition
e   a champion
f   a professional sports person
g   a medal

5 **Complete the sentences with the words and phrases in the box.**

away matches   home matches
live matches   season tickets

1 It's usually easier for fans to get to _____ .

2 Fans usually have to travel further to watch _____ .

3 _____ cost a lot but getting one is cheaper than paying every time if you go to lots of matches.

4 It is more exciting to watch _____ in a stadium than recorded ones on TV.

6 Complete the text with *do, play* or *go*.

I love sports! I work in a sports centre as a tennis coach, so I **¹**_____ tennis every day. I also **²**_____ yoga every day, in the morning before breakfast. On Monday and Wednesday evenings, I **³**_____ volleyball. At the weekends in the summer, I go to my dad's house by the sea, and we **⁴**_____ sailing or windsurfing if the weather is OK. In the winter, we **⁵**_____ snowboarding in the mountains most weekends. I'd like to **⁶**_____ judo as well, but I'm too busy!

GRAMMAR

1 Complete the sentences with the correct form of the words given.

must/can

1 We _____ play on the club's pitch if we finish at 6 pm.

2 Players _____ be at the club at least 10 minutes before the bus leaves at 8.30 am.

have to/can

3 For a match, the basketball _____ be the right size and type.

4 The players _____ get free match tickets for their families.

need to/can

5 Karl _____ practise hitting the ball harder.

6 People of all ages and levels _____ join our yoga class.

not have to/mustn't

7 You _____ wear football boots in the gym because it's bad for the floor.

8 Players _____ buy their kit. The club buys it for them.

can't/not need to

9 Children who are over 14 years old _____ be with an adult.

10 You _____ swim here because it is a fishing lake.

2 Choose the correct answer and write it in the gap in the text.

I love playing tennis. I **¹**_____ twice a week and there is usually a match on Saturdays, too. If the coach chooses me for the team, I **²**_____ this Saturday. I **³**_____ tennis since I was about six. My dad **⁴**_____ me to play when we **⁵**_____ in Paris. We live in Milan now because Dad **⁶**_____ in a bank here for two years, but after that we **⁷**_____ probably go to another country. The great thing about tennis is that people play it nearly everywhere!

1	am practising	practise	practised
2	play	will play	was playing
3	played	am going to play	have played
4	taught	has taught	teaches
5	are living	have lived	were living
6	works	is working	worked
7	are going to	will	did

PUSH YOURSELF / B1

Complete the text with the adverbs in the box.

| after | afterwards | always | finally |
| fortunately | suddenly | unfortunately | |

I **¹**_____ go to the gym on Tuesday evening. **²**_____ I get home from college, I get my sports bag with my gym kit and towel in it, and walk down the road to the gym near my house. It was Tuesday yesterday, so when I got home, I went to get my sports bag but I couldn't find it anywhere. I spent a long time looking for it, but **³**_____ gave up. I sat down in the kitchen and started to think about where it could be. I thought about going to the gym last Tuesday. **⁴**_____ I remembered where my bag was – in my brother's car. He brought me home from the gym last Tuesday and then went to stay with his fiancé **⁵**_____ . But **⁶**_____ , he's still at his fiancé's house, 200 kilometres away! So last night I had to borrow some gym clothes from my mum. **⁷**_____ , we wear the same size of clothes and trainers. But our styles are very different. I've never felt so NOT cool!

LISTENING PART 5

 18 For each question, choose the correct answer. You will hear Steve talking to a friend about his family and sports. What sport does each person do?

Example Steve ☐ C

PEOPLE		**SPORTS**	
1	sister ☐	**A**	athletics
2	brother ☐	**B**	basketball
3	granddad ☐	**C**	cricket
4	mum ☐	**D**	football
5	dad ☐	**E**	racket sports
		F	rugby
		G	swimming
		H	volleyball

READING

1 **Read the text. What is the best title for it?**

- **A** A life in sport
- **B** Life in a sporty family
- **C** Life after professional sports

A Rachel Atherton is a professional mountain-bike rider. She is also part of an amazing family. Rachel has been a mountain-bike world champion four times and her two older brothers, Gee and Dan, have also been world champions in the same sport.

B The Atherton family is from Wales. It was there that sport became a large part of Rachel and her brothers' lives when they began riding their bikes in the hills and fields near their house. Rachel began riding a BMX bike when she was eight years old and mountain bikes when she was 11. She became national youth champion of down-hill mountain biking for the first time when she was 15 and world champion for the first time when she was 21.

C For many years, Rachel and her brothers have toured the world together to do their sport. As well as going to competitions, they spend the winter in California, USA, where they train for the race season.

D But mountain biking is not the only sport that Rachel does. When she is in California, she trains on other kinds of bikes which help make her stronger. Rachel also goes to the gym as part of her training, and does yoga every evening. She says the yoga is a very important part of keeping her body healthy and strong. It also helps her body get better again after a hard race.

E Being a professional mountain-bike rider is very tiring and stressful, so she enjoys going home to Wales to relax. Of course, for Rachel, this does not mean sitting on the sofa watching TV. She usually goes hill walking or does a water sport such as kayaking.

2 **Read the text again. In which paragraph can you find the following information?**

1	something Rachel does each day
2	what Rachel's job is
3	where Rachel grew up
4	the travelling that Rachel has to do to be the best at her sport
5	the first type of bike she rode
6	what Rachel does when she isn't training
7	which activities help Rachel keep fit
8	the reason why her family is special
9	how Rachel's job makes her feel
10	when she won some important competitions

Match the questions (1-6) with the answers (a-f).

1 Would you like to be a professional footballer?
2 Why do people do sport?
3 Which sports do you like best?
4 What do you think of cricket?
5 Do you play any sports?
6 Do you prefer watching sports or doing sports?

a It's good for us.
b It looks a bit boring!
c I'd love to!
d Yes, I do judo.
e I like doing sports much more.
f My favourite sport is basketball.

WRITING

1 Put the words in the correct order to make sentences.

0 her dog / Maria / ran away. / was looking at her phone / While
While Maria was looking at her phone, her dog ran away.

1 was playing his guitar / Richard / arrived with a box. / when / his aunt

2 Nick / As / it / was driving along the street / started to snow.

3 was shining / Lucy's race / when / began. / The sun

4 were walking through the park / Two children / when / started to follow them. / a little kitten

5 started to eat their picnic. / the family were swimming in the sea / some birds / While

2 Write the sentences from Exercise 1 again as the beginning of stories. Add the words given for each sentence.

0 young / One day / black and white
One day, while Maria was looking at her phone, her young black and white dog ran away.

1 large / new / favourite / One afternoon

2 One evening / dark

3 important / Last Saturday / long-distance

4 young / Yesterday / sweet

5 delicious / annoying / Last weekend

ANSWER KEY

STARTER

VOCABULARY

Exercise 1
1 grandfather
2 niece
3 husband
4 daughter
5 uncle
6 cousin
7 child
8 sister
9 grandparent
10 grandma/granny
11 dad/father
12 granddaughter

Exercise 2
1 (north) American
2 Mexico
3 Portuguese
4 France, Canadian
5 China
6 Italian
7 Spain

Exercise 3
1 076953221
2 25th July 2002
3 21
4 2024
5 290
6 SW14 8GM

Exercise 4
1 driving licence
2 passport
3 identity card
4 first name, surname
5 DOB

GRAMMAR

Exercise 1
A am, 'm/am, Are, 's/is
   Correct order: 4,2,3,1
B aren't/are not, 're/are, are, 'm/am, Are
   Correct order: 2,3,1
C 's/is, isn't/'s not/is not, 's/is, 're/are, 's/is, Is
   Correct order: 4 2 3 1

Exercise 2
1 Tanya's
2 Mike's
3 Nihal's
4 name's/is
5 Nick's car's/car is

Exercise 3
1 Dean has got/'s got a/one brother.
2 Dean's parents have got two sons.
3 Dean's parents haven't got a big house.
4 Dean has got/'s got a motorbike.
5 Dean hasn't got a car.

Exercise 4
1 Carla can swim one kilometre.
2 Roberto can't swim one kilometre.
3 Roberto and Carla can speak Spanish.
4 Carla can't cook paella.
5 Roberto can cook paella.
6 Roberto and Carla can write computer programs.

Exercise 5
1 does, come
2 doesn't live
3 lives
4 Does he work
5 does
6 works
7 doesn't
8 Does he speak
9 loves

LISTENING

Exercise 1
1 T, R, K, S, H, I, U
2 H, S, I, N, C, E, E

Exercise 2
1 Turkish
2 Chinese

Exercise 3
1 1st May 2018
2 31st August 1992
3 20th September 2004
4 15th March 2025

Exercise 4
1 Chinese
2 Lucy
3 Mansfield
4 2nd June
5 American
6 58 Charnwood
7 0795301244

READING

Exercise 1
1 B   3 A
2 D   4 C

Exercise 2
1 Mexico
2 Italian
3 USA
4 20 years old
5 fish
6 art

SPEAKING

Exercise 1
1 C
2 C
3 A
4 B
5 B
6 C

Exercise 2
1
Q: What's your first name?
A: Patricia.
2
Q: How old are you?
A: I'm twenty.
3
Q: What's your job?
A: I'm an actor.
4
Q: Where do you come from?
A: I'm Italian.
5
Q: How many brothers and sisters have you got?
A: One of each.
6
Q: Where do you live?
A: In Paris, France.

WRITING
1 is/'s
2 has got/'s got
3 's/is
4 doesn't live
5 speaks/can speak
6 's/is
7 's got/has got

UNIT 1

VOCABULARY

Exercise 1
1 wake up
2 stay
3 get up
4 have
5 get dressed
6 have
7 get on
8 take off
9 put on

Exercise 2
1 after
2 before
3 before
4 after
5 after
6 before

Exercise 3
1 (a) quarter to five
2 (a) quarter past six
3 11 o'clock
4 half past one

Exercise 4
a 6
b 3
c 2
d 4
e 1
f 5

GRAMMAR

Exercise 1
1 are
2 works
3 am
4 start
5 don't get up
6 get up
7 doesn't like
8 have
9 doesn't eat
10 has

Exercise 2
1 Does Natalie work
2 Do the sisters/they get up
3 Does Mischa like
4 Does Mischa stay
5 Do the sisters/they have
6 Does Natalie have

Exercise 3
1 C
2 A
3 C
4 B
5 A
6 C

Exercise 4
1 do, want to do, want to go
2 does. want to be, wants to travel
3 does, want to do, doesn't want to get, wants to win
4 do, want to work, want to work

Exercise 5

1 Stefi likes going out dancing on Friday evenings.
2 Louis doesn't like staying in bed after he wakes up.
3 Leo and Tom like playing computer games together.
4 My mum and I love swimming in the sea.
5 Johnnie hates going shopping at the supermarket.
6 My English teacher doesn't like working in hot weather.

LISTENING

Exercise 1

	Kenny	Zadie
A	4	6
B	3	1
C	1	2
D	2	4
E	5	5
F	6	3

Exercise 2

1 Kenny
2 Zadie
3 Kenny
4 Zadie
5 Zadie

READING PART 2

1 C   5 B
2 B   6 C
3 A   7 A
4 C

PUSH YOURSELF B1

1 ✗   4 ✗
2 ✗   5 ✔
3 ✔

SPEAKING

[Suggested answers]

1 Where do you work? I work at a newspaper office.
2 How do you go/get/travel to work? I go to work by bus.
3 When do you get to work? I get to work at 8.00 am.
4 Why do you like your job? I like my job because I like meeting interesting people.
5 Who do you live with? I live with three friends.

WRITING

1 Dear
2 wishes
3 Hi
4 Love from
5 the best

UNIT 2
VOCABULARY

Exercise 1

1 January
2 September
3 July
4 March
5 June
6 October
7 December

Exercise 2

1 summer   3 winter
2 autumn   4 spring

Exercise 3

1 ice
2 stormy, lightning
3 temperature
4 cloud, rain
5 sunny
6 foggy
7 snowy

Exercise 4

A a lake
B a mountain
C a coast
D a valley
E a waterfall
F an island
G a desert
H a forest

GRAMMAR

Exercise 1

1 'm/am wearing
2 's/is snowing
3 're not/aren't studying
4 're/are talking
5 're/are leaving
6 aren't going

Exercise 2

1 What are you doing there?
2 We're working here this week.
3 Are you staying in a hotel?
4 I am having a great week!
5 So I'm not working.
6 Where are you staying?
7 Some friends are visiting us at the moment.

Exercise 3

1 'm/am having, have
2 enjoys, 's/is enjoying
3 lives, 's/is living
4 are playing, play
5 drives, 's/is driving
6 rains, 's/is raining

READING

Exercise 1

B

Exercise 2

1 conservation officer
2 south
3 South America, Africa
4 smaller islands
5 visitors
6 the weather/temperature/climate

PUSH YOURSELF B1

1 heavy
2 strong
3 thick
4 bright, clear
5 hard

LISTENING PART 1

1 C   4 B
2 A   5 C
3 C

SPEAKING

Exercise 1

1 there's
2 Maybe
3 sitting
4 in the middle
5 it's
6 are enjoying
7 aren't wearing
8 see
9 below

Exercise 2

What is there in the photo?
Sentence number: 1
Describing details
Sentence number: 7, 8
What is happening in the photo?
Sentence number: 3
The weather in the photo
Sentence number: 5
Where are things in the photo?
Sentence number: 4, 9
What do you think?
Sentence number: 2, 6

WRITING

Exercise 1

Do you want to come with us?
how about staying at our house tonight?
would you like to bring a friend with you?

Exercise 2

1 I'd love to come but I'm afraid I've got football practice from 4 pm–6.30 pm.
2 That would be wonderful.
3 Thanks for asking but all my friends are busy tomorrow.

UNIT 3
VOCABULARY

Exercise 1

1 blogger
2 upload
3 social media
4 comments
5 series
6 episode
7 download
8 stream

Exercise 2

1 news
2 documentary
3 crime drama
4 comedy
5 quiz show
6 action film

Exercise 3

1 a   4 b
2 e   5 d
3 c

It's a science-fiction film.

GRAMMAR

Exercise 1

1 were
2 wasn't
3 Were, were
4 was
5 weren't
6 were

Exercise 2

1 Did … watch, played
2 did … decide, loved
3 did … finish, didn't work
4 helped, Did … enjoy

Exercise 3

1 spoke to her uncle
2 went shopping
3 got up at 10 o'clock
4 had breakfast in/at a café

READING PART 3

1 C   4 A
2 C   5 C
3 B

Exercise 1

1 enjoyable, amusing
2 amusing, silly
3 awful, disappointing
4 dull, uninteresting

Exercise 2

1 true   4 false
2 false   5 true
3 false

LISTENING

Exercise 1

1 the weather on Saturday
2 different kinds of TV
3 doing something with family members
4 an outside activity

Exercise 2

1 Anna   4 Ryan
2 Anna   5 Anna
3 Ryan   6 Ryan

SPEAKING

Exercise 1

1 How was your weekend?
2 What did you get up to last night?
3 Did you have a good weekend?
4 What do you do on Friday afternoons?
5 Do you usually go shopping on Saturdays?

Exercise 2

A 4   D 1
B 5   E 2
C 3

Exercise 3

1 d   4 c
2 b
3 a

WRITING

1 The setting is
2 The story is about
3 The plot is
4 My favourite character is
5 My favourite moment is
6 The best things about the film are

UNIT 4
VOCABULARY

Exercise 1

1 false – five toes
2 true
3 true
4 true
5 true
6 false – in the middle of your legs
7 true
8 false – part of your hand(s)

Exercise 2

1 brain   4 back
2 neck   5 knees
3 fingers

Exercise 3

1 dentist, toothache
2 medicine, pharmacy
3 sick, fine
4 hospital, leg

GRAMMAR

Exercise 1

1 can   4 can't
2 couldn't 5 couldn't
3 could   6 could

Exercise 2

1 Can Leah ride a motorbike?
2 Can Leah swim 1,000 metres / drive a car
3 Could Leah ride a horse
4 Could Leah swim 1,000 metres / drive a car

Exercise 3

1 shouldn't 5 should
2 should   6 shouldn't
3 shouldn't 7 should
4 should   8 Should

1 (on your) wrist
2 (your) lungs
3 (the) ankle
4 (the) hips
5 (your) elbow
6 (your) muscles

LISTENING PART 2

1 Tuesday(s)
2 7.00
3 6/six
4 forest
5 picnic

READING

Exercise 1

D, E

Exercise 2

1 fly   5 field
2 foot   6 leg
3 office   7 towel
4 finger   8 wrist

SPEAKING

Exercise 1

1 Are you OK?
2 better
3 how's
4 How are you?
5 sorry to hear that
6 What's the matter

Exercise 2

1 d   4 a
2 b   5 e
3 f   6 c

WRITING

1 One day
2 suddenly
3 then
4 After that

UNIT 5
VOCABULARY

Exercise 1

1 a flight
2 a traveller
3 street food
4 catch a train
5 go to work
6 a national park

Exercise 2

1 backpacks, luggage
2 miss, delay
3 accommodation, tent
4 tour guide, tourist information centre

Exercise 3

1 journey
2 flight
3 trip
4 travel
5 cruise
6 crossing

GRAMMAR

Exercise 1

1 was reading
2 wasn't listening
3 were watching
4 Were … camping
5 Was … raining
6 weren't looking
7 Were … winning

Exercise 2

1 was reading, was sitting
2 booked
3 was packing, called
4 was packing, found
5 asked, was looking
6 was looking, found

READING PART 4

Exercise 1

1 Paragraph 2
2 Paragraph 1
3 Paragraph 2
4 Paragraph 2
5 Paragraph 1
6 Paragraph 1

Exercise 2

1 C   4 B
2 B   5 A
3 A   6 C

LISTENING

Exercise 1

A 4
B 5
C 1
D 3
E 2

Exercise 2

1 B   4 C
2 B   5 A
3 A

PUSH YOURSELF B1

1	C	4	B
2	D	5	A
3	F	6	E

SPEAKING

Exercise 1

a	5	d	2
b	4	e	1
c	6	f	3

Exercise 2

1	enjoy	4	terrible
2	had	5	for me
3	fantastic	6	think

WRITING

1 This morning
2 Right now
3 while
4 Yesterday
5 after that
6 the evening

UNIT 6
VOCABULARY

Exercise 1

A an omelette
B a chicken
C some cereal
D a beef curry
E some broccoli
F a mango
G some mushrooms
H some yoghurt

Exercise 2

1 Starters
2 Main courses
3 Desserts
4 Lunch
5 Dinner

Exercise 3

1 yoghurt, ice cream
2 chocolate
3 soup, cereal
4 eggs

GRAMMAR

Exercise 1

1	some	5	any
2	some	6	any
3	any	7	a
4	an	8	a

Exercise 2

how many: apple, biscuit, burger
how much: rice, salt, bread
a little: rice, salt, bread
a few: apple, biscuit, burger
not much: rice, salt, bread
not many: apple, biscuit, burger
a lot of: apple, rice, biscuit, burger, salt, bread

Exercise 3

1 How many (packets of) crisps does Nadya eat? A lot.
2 How much meat does Nadya eat? Not much.
3 How much chocolate does Martin eat? / How many bars of chocolate does Martin eat? Not much. / Not many.
4 How many eggs does Nadya eat? Not many.

Exercise 4

1 doesn't drink much
2 eats a lot of
3 doesn't eat much
4 eats a lot of
5 doesn't eat many

LISTENING PART 5

1	G	4	A
2	C	5	H
3	B		

PUSH YOURSELF B1

1 peel
2 Chop
3 Peel
4 Fry
5 stir
6 add
7 add
8 burn
9 Grill
10 Steam

READING

Exercise 1

B

Exercise 2

1	F	4	F	7	F
2	T	5	T	8	F
3	T	6	F		

SPEAKING

Exercise 1

1	go	4	ask
2	having	5	paying
3	eating		

Exercise 2

1 shall
2 How about
3 I'm afraid
4 Let's
5 That's a good idea
6 I don't mind
7 Shall

WRITING

1	First	5	until
2	Then	6	While
3	After	7	Next
4	when	8	Finally

UNIT 7
VOCABULARY

Exercise 1

1 baking
2 doing photography
3 going to the gym
4 hanging out with friends
5 playing board games
6 going to gigs
7 doing Massaoke
8 doing exercise

Exercise 2

1	e	3	c	5	d
2	b	4	a		

Exercise 3

1	flute	4	piano
2	drums	5	keyboard
3	violin	6	trumpets

Exercise 4

1 songwriter
2 musician
3 solo artist
4 drummer
5 singer
6 guitarist
(answers in any order) Ed is a songwriter, a musician, a solo artist, a singer and a guitarist.

GRAMMAR

Exercise 1

1 Has Joe ever won a game of chess?
Yes, he has.
2 Have Max and Joe ever lived near a desert?
No, they haven't.
3 Have Max and Joe ever visited a country in Africa?
Yes, they have.
4 Has Joe ever spoken to a famous person?
Yes, he has.
5 Have Max and Joe ever been to a gig together?
No, they haven't.

Exercise 2

1 has won
2 have never lived
3 have visited
4 has never spoken
5 have never been

Exercise 3

1 He's just driven into the garage.
2 Because she's just run up some stairs.
3 I've just found it on the desk.
4 They've just left their flat!

LISTENING

Exercise 1

1	C	2	B

Exercise 2

1	C	3	C	5	B
2	A	4	A	6	C

READING PART 1

1	A	3	B	5	C
2	B	4	B	6	A

PUSH YOURSELF B1

1	A	5	B
2	B	6	B
3	A	7	A
4	B	8	A

SPEAKING

Exercise 1

1 Because it makes me feel fantastic!
2 I think it's important to learn new things.
3 It helps to relax me/me to relax after a busy day at work.
4 It makes me feel like a rock star!
5 I think it helps me to be a stronger person.

Exercise 2

1	e	3	c	5	d
2	f	4	a	6	b

WRITING

Exercise 1

1 isn't
2 know
3 is
4 doesn't mean
5 is something
6 isn't
7 is
8 isn't
9 enjoyed
10 was

Exercise 2

1 delicious
2 Special
3 world-famous
4 traditional
5 amazing
6 excellent

UNIT 8
VOCABULARY

Exercise 1

1 villa
2 cottage
3 townhouse
4 houseboat
5 studio flat
6 apartment

Exercise 2

1 ground
2 building
3 balcony
4 furniture
5 roof
6 neighbours
7 views
8 garage
9 basement
10 rent

Exercise 3

1 fridge
2 oven
3 cooker
4 cupboard
5 tap
6 sink

Exercise 4

1 a rug
2 stairs
3 a shelf
4 curtains
5 a lamp
6 a sofa

GRAMMAR

Exercise 1

1 's/has already had a shower.
2 haven't/have not arrived at work yet.
3 haven't/have not left the house yet.
4 've/have already eaten.
5 hasn't/has not finished the exam yet.
6 've/have already met him.
7 's/has already bought three.
8 haven't found one they like yet.

Exercise 2

since: June, this morning, 12 o'clock
for: 10 years, five minutes, a few hours

Exercise 3

1 finished, hasn't been
2 found, has/'s rented
3 have … had, bought
4 did … go, didn't go
5 have known, met
6 has/'s been, have/'ve lived

PUSH YOURSELF B1

Exercise 1

1 forgotten, kind of
2 how to, keep
3 it's called but, use it for
4 the English word, part of

Exercise 2

1 sofa/bench
2 cupboard/fridge
3 oven/cooker
4 basement/cellar

LISTENING PART 4

1	C	4	A
2	B	5	B
3	B		

READING

Exercise 1

A, C, D, E, F

Exercise 2

Paragraph 1 B
Paragraph 2 A
Paragraph 3 C
Paragraph 4 B
Paragraph 5 C
Paragraph 6 A

SPEAKING

Exercise 1

1 home
2 part
3 anything
4 best
5 describe

Exercise 2

a	south	d	cafés
b	floor	e	tiles
c	noisy		

Exercise 3

1	b	4	d
2	a	5	e
3	c		

WRITING

Exercise 1

1	e	4	b
2	f	5	a
3	d	6	c

Exercise 2

1 My new apartment
2 Hello
3 How are you?
4 I'm writing to tell you
5 near

6 at
7 I wanted to ask you
8 All the best

UNIT 9
VOCABULARY

Exercise 1

1	b	4	e	7	f
2	c	5	a		
3	g	6	d		

Exercise 2

1 good mood
2 worried
3 angry
4 bad mood
5 get on well
6 argue
7 get on badly

Exercise 3

1 happy
2 exciting
3 easy
4 decide
5 ask
6 agree
7 prefer
8 teach
9 want

GRAMMAR

Exercise 1

1 hated/hates working
2 enjoys riding
3 before eating
4 started playing
5 after watching
6 at writing
7 without paying

Exercise 2

1 to play
2 playing
3 to play
4 to play
5 having
6 to go
7 playing
8 to book
9 not to forget

PUSH YOURSELF B1

1 don't mind
2 be bothered
3 feel like
4 excited about
5 hoping
6 am planning

LISTENING PART 3

1	B	3	C	5	A
2	A	4	B		

READING PART 5

Exercise 1

1	at	4	What
2	an	5	all
3	am/'m	6	to

Exercise 2

1	T	4	T	7	F
2	F	5	F		
3	T	6	F		

SPEAKING

1 don't you write
2 should/could look on
3 turning it off / turning off your phone
4 shouldn't go to
5 about preparing
6 him to listen to
7 idea to cycle

WRITING

1 for your email
2 It was great
3 How about joining
4 It's not expensive
5 I'd like to ask you
6 Could you tell me
7 hear from you soon
8 Best wishes

UNIT 10
VOCABULARY

Exercise 1

1 fountains
2 library
3 theatre
4 castle
5 department store
6 statue
7 stadium

Exercise 2

1	don't go	5	aren't
2	are	6	shouldn't
3	aren't	7	can
4	need		

Exercise 3

1 roundabout
2 crossing
3 underground station
4 traffic light
5 bus stop
6 corner

Exercise 4

1	Excuse	6	Take
2	know	7	go
3	walk	8	tell
4	turn	9	get
5	give	10	see

GRAMMAR

Exercise 1

1	won't	6	won't
2	may	7	might not
3	won't	8	might
4	'll/will	9	'll/will
5	may not	10	might

Exercise 2

1 'll be
2 'll chop
3 Shall … make
4 'll look
5 Shall … go
6 'll stay
7 'll drive
8 Shall … get
9 'll see

PUSH YOURSELF B1

1 Public transport
2 skyscraper
3 historic
4 traffic-free
5 polluted
6 pavements
7 pedestrians
8 traffic jams

LISTENING PART 2

1	station	4	4th/fourth
2	15th	5	pen
3	8.30		

READING

Exercise 1

A, C, D, E

Exercise 2

1	C	4	E
2	B	5	A
3	F		

SPEAKING

1	B, C	5	B, C
2	B, C	6	A, B
3	A, C	7	B, C
4	A, B		

WRITING

a I'll never forget seeing that fantastic view of the city.
b It was great to meet him.
c I had a wonderful day.
d It's the most amazing market I've ever been to.
e My favourite moment was when we arrived at the top.
f I'm looking forward to showing you the city.

1	c
2	d
3	e
4	a
5	f
6	b

UNIT 11
VOCABULARY

Exercise 1

1 reduced items
2 receipt
3 sale
4 bill
5 salary
6 discounts

Exercise 2

1	borrowed	5	earn
2	cost	6	wasted
3	saved	7	paid
4	spent	8	lent

Exercise 3

1	b	3	e	5	g	7	d
2	f	4	c	6	a		

GRAMMAR

Exercise 1

1 leaves
2 does … close
3 starts
4 do … arrive

Exercise 2

1 are taking
2 is not/isn't/'s not going
3 am/'m working
4 does … stop
5 are … meeting
6 start

Exercise 3

1 doing/going to do
2 is getting married
3 is playing
4 are/'re staying/going

to stay

5 are you going to spend
6 'm/am going to save
7 'm/am going to buy

READING

Exercise 1

B, C

Exercise 2

1 (boxes of) strawberries
2 strawberries, tomatoes
3 angry (and stupid)
4 (some) blogs
5 more often
6 in the fridge
7 world

PUSH YOURSELF B1

1 bank account
2 afford
3 owes
4 on credit
5 second-hand
6 bargains
7 worth
8 value for money

LISTENING PART 1

1	C	4	A
2	B	5	C
3	B		

SPEAKING

Exercise 1

1 as/because, old and dirty
2 because/as, really boring
3 lovely little, That's why
4 delicious, so

Exercise 2

1	c
2	d
3	a
4	b

WRITING

1 near
2 building
3 One of the best
4 Another good
5 high point
6 bargains
7 One bad
8 Another negative
9 the worst thing
10 All in all
11 wouldn't recommend
12 go back

UNIT 12
VOCABULARY

Exercise 1
1. biology
2. geography
3. physics
4. history
5. drama
6. maths
7. chemistry

Exercise 2
[Suggested answers]
1. history, geography, modern languages
2. maths, physics
3. geography, physics
4. physics
5. drama
6. history, modern languages
7. history, geography, physics

Exercise 3
1. secondary school
2. a qualification
3. graduate
4. get good marks
5. a degree
6. primary school

Exercise 4
1. Are … revising/studying
2. revising/studying
3. pass
4. fail
5. take

Exercise 5
1. diploma
2. long hours
3. break
4. boss
5. day off
6. staff

GRAMMAR

Exercise 1
1. If I eat fish, I feel ill.
2. Plants die if they don't have water.
3. The room is too hot if you close the windows.
4. Phones sometimes break if you drop them.
5. If we go to Rome, we can visit my family there.
6. Cars get very dirty if you don't clean them.

Exercise 2
1. e If the train arrives late at the airport, we'll miss our flight.
2. f You won't have enough money for the video game if I don't lend you some.
3. b If you have any questions during the tour, the guide will try to answer them.
4. d If the mangoes in the supermarket are very small, I won't buy any.
5. a We'll go to the cinema if it rains on holiday.
6. c Bernardo will win the whole competition if he wins another game.

Exercise 3
1. was built
2. are made
3. were told
4. was enjoyed by
5. is visited by
6. are taken

LISTENING PART 4
1. B
2. A
3. B
4. A
5. C

PUSH YOURSELF B1
1. unless
2. When
3. unless
4. if
5. Unless
6. If
7. When

READING

Exercise 1
C

Exercise 2
1. e
2. g
3. d
4. c
5. a
6. i

SPEAKING

Exercise 1
1. Person applying for job
2. Interviewer
3. Person applying for job
4. Person applying for job
5. Person applying for job
6. Interviewer
7. Person applying for job
8. Interviewer
9. Person applying for job
10. Person applying for job

Exercise 2
a. 4
b. 6
c. 7
d. 5
e. 10
f. 8
g. 9
h. 1
i. 2
j. 3

WRITING
1. I am writing to apply for the job of waiter as advertised in your café.
2. I am attaching/attach/have attached my CV with my qualifications and experience.
3. As you will see/As you can see from my CV, I have worked/worked in another café for a year and I have a diploma in business studies.
4. I am always very friendly and polite.
5. I look forward to hearing from you.

UNIT 13
VOCABULARY

Exercise 1
1. c
2. b
3. a
4. e
5. d

Exercise 2
1. brilliant
2. confident
3. annoying
4. sweet
5. quiet
6. Sociable
7. lazy
8. kind

Exercise 3
1. sporty
2. cool
3. fashionable
4. smart
5. casual

Exercise 4
1. handbag
2. sandals
3. tie
4. jewellery
5. sunglasses
6. suits
7. trainers

GRAMMAR

Exercise 1
1. What does he look like?
2. What 's/is she like?
3. What are they like?
4. What does she look like?

Exercise 2
1. shorter than
2. thinner than
3. better looking / more good looking than
4. happier than
5. worse than
6. more boring than

Exercise 3
1. the hottest
2. the ugliest
3. the sweetest
4. the most interesting
5. the most expensive
6. the best
7. the worst

LISTENING PART 3
1. C
2. B
3. A
4. B
5. C

PUSH YOURSELF B1
1. is as clever as
2. is as high as
3. wasn't as warm as
4. isn't as good as
5. isn't as expensive as
6. isn't as easy as

READING
1. C
2. D
3. A
4. F
5. E
6. B

SPEAKING
1. 're wearing
2. 've got
3. think
4. sure
5. Perhaps/Maybe
6. probably
7. don't think
8. looks
9. Maybe/Perhaps
10. could be

WRITING

Exercise 1

Paragraph 1: C
Paragraph 2: D
Paragraph 3: A
Paragraph 4: B

Exercise 2

1 On the less positive side
2 So do I recommend the tent?
3 it depends on what you want.
4 then it is not a good buy
5 I fell in love with
6 It's the coolest tent
7 But for me, the best thing

UNIT 14
VOCABULARY

Exercise 1

1 athletics
2 basketball
3 cricket
4 rugby
5 tennis
6 football

Exercise 2

1 F football
2 F football
3 T
4 F basketball
5 F athletics
6 T
7 T
8 F tennis

Exercise 3

1 pitch
2 referee
3 red card
4 sent off
5 rules
6 lose

Exercise 4

1 g
2 b
3 e
4 a
5 f
6 c
7 d

Exercise 5

1 home matches
2 away matches
3 Season tickets
4 live matches

Exercise 6

1 play   4 go
2 do   5 go
3 play   6 do

GRAMMAR

Exercise 1

1 can
2 must
3 has to
4 can
5 needs to
6 can
7 mustn't
8 don't have to
9 don't need to
10 can't

Exercise 2

1 practise
2 will play
3 have played
4 taught
5 were living
6 is working
7 will

PUSH YOURSELF B1

1 always
2 After
3 finally
4 Suddenly
5 afterwards
6 unfortunately
7 Fortunately

LISTENING PART 5

1 H   4 G
2 A   5 D
3 E

READING

Exercise 1

A

Exercise 2

1 D   6 E
2 A   7 D
3 B   8 A
4 C   9 E
5 B   10 B

SPEAKING

1 c   4 b
2 a   5 d
3 f   6 e

WRITING

Exercise 1

1 Richard was playing his guitar when his aunt arrived with a box.
2 As Nick was driving along the street, it started to snow.
3 The sun was shining when Lucy's race began.
4 Two children were walking through the park when a little kitten started to follow them.
5 While the family were swimming in the sea, some birds started to eat their picnic.

Exercise 2

1 One afternoon, Richard was playing his (favourite) new guitar when his (favourite) aunt arrived with a large box.
2 One evening, as Nick was driving along the dark street, it started to snow.
3 Last Saturday, the sun was shining when Lucy's important long-distance race began.
4 Yesterday, two young children were walking through the park when a sweet little kitten started to follow them.
5 Last weekend while the family were swimming in the sea, some annoying birds started to eat their delicious picnic.

AUDIOSCRIPT

STARTER

🔊 **Track 02**

1   T, R, K, S, H, I, U
2   H, S, I, N, C, E, E

🔊 **Track 03**

1   The first of May twenty eighteen
2   The thirty-first of August 1992
3   The twentieth of September 2004
4   The fifteenth of March twenty twenty-five

🔊 **Track 04**

Man: Good morning, welcome to the Art School.

Woman: Thanks. I'd like to join one of your evening art courses.

Man: OK. Which one?

Woman: It's the Chinese writing course. I can speak the language, but I want to learn to paint the writing. It's so beautiful.

Man: Yes, it is. Very beautiful. So I need to ask you some questions to fill in this form.

Woman: OK.

Man: What's your first name, please?

Woman: It's Lucy. L-U-C-Y.

Man: OK. And your surname?

Woman: Mansfield. That's M-A-N-S-F-I-E-L-D.

Man: Thank you. And what's your date of birth, please?

Woman: It's the second of June, 2001.

Man: Great. Next question … What's your nationality?

Woman: Well I live and work here in England, but actually I'm American.

Man: OK. Good, only two questions now. Can you tell me your address?

Woman: Yes, it's 58 Charnwood Road.

Man: How do you spell that?

Woman: It's C-H-A-R-N-W-O-O-D.

Man: Fine. And lastly, your phone number please.

Woman: Right, it's 0795301244.

Man: Thanks. Now. I'll give you some information …

UNIT 1

🔊 **Track 05**

Man: The best thing about my working life is that every day is different. I travel a lot, but when I'm at home I like getting up early. The first thing I do is to take my dog for a walk. I think that's the perfect start to a day – being outside in the sun. Then I take the dog home and go out to the café near my house for a coffee. Back home again, I have a shower, get dressed and go to the computer to start work. After answering some emails, I talk to people about the jobs I'm doing with them, then write. At the end of the day, my favourite thing to do is go swimming at the pool near my house.

Woman: I don't like to get out of bed quickly in the morning. When I hear the alarm clock at about seven o'clock, I wake up and my husband brings me a cup of green tea – my favourite drink. He always gets up before me. I feel awake after the tea, so then I'm ready to get up and go for a swim in the sea – our house is next to the beach. I usually go for a walk along the beach after my swim, too. Then it's time to go to the computer and start my day's work. But before I start, I always speak to my friends and family on the phone.

UNIT 2

🔊 **Track 06**

Listening Part 1

Narrator: For each question, choose the correct answer. Now we are ready to start. Look at question one. What weather does Maria's island usually have in March?

Man: What's the weather like on your island at the moment, Maria?

Woman: It's warm and sunny, which is lovely. But it's very different from the weather we usually have in March. Most years there are strong winds and lots of rain during this month.

Man: Really? Well we've still got snow here in the mountains.

Woman: Oh great!

Narrator: Now listen again.

Narrator: Two. Where is the man's uncle travelling now?

Man: My uncle's having a great time travelling around the world.

Woman: Really? Where is he at the moment?

Man: He left his home in the USA in April, and then went to South America for six months last year. But at the moment he's in Africa. He loves it there, and is driving across a desert this week. He'll come to Europe after that, I think.

Woman: Sounds great.

Narrator: Now listen again.

Narrator: Three. In which month does Monica stay with her grandparents?

Man: What do you do in the summer holidays, Monica?

Woman: I stay in the city in June and July – I work in a shop. Then I go back to my family in the country in August. I stay with my grandparents and help on their farm. What about you?

Man: I work in my aunt's hotel in June, July and August.

Narrator: Now listen again.

Narrator: Four. Where is Richard working this week?

Woman: Are you enjoying your job in the national park, Richard?

Man: It's fantastic. We do something different every week. Last week we worked on the island in the lake, but now we're cleaning the waterfall in the river. Other staff are cutting the long grass on the hill this week so we can put some animals there next week.

Woman: Wow! That's amazing.

Narrator: Now listen again.

Narrator: Five. What is Jessica's friend, Lucy, doing in the forest?

Man: Are you going for a run today, Jessica?

Woman: No, because I usually run with Lucy, and she's busy. She's taking her son for a walk.

Man: Is she? Why don't you go with her? Where are they going?

Woman: In the forest. She invited me, but I'm going to go for a ride on my bike instead.

Narrator: Now listen again.

Narrator: That is the end of Part One.

UNIT 3

🔊 Track 07

Anna: What did you do on Saturday, Ryan?

Ryan: I went to my cousin's house, on the coast. It was good to get out of the city because it was so hot.

Anna: I know. The temperature was 38 degrees! I stayed in the city and didn't go out. I downloaded a TV series and watched that.

Ryan: Cool! So which series was it?

Anna: A science-fiction series called *White Sky*. Do you know it?

Ryan: Yes, but I don't like that kind of series very much. I prefer crime drama.

Anna: Really? I think that's so dull – every series is the same!

Ryan: Not really! Some are quite scary, and some are really clever. So did you do anything else on Saturday?

Anna: Yes, I played a video game with my dad. I thought it was a bit boring, but he enjoyed it.

Ryan: I played a new video game with my cousin and it was brilliant!

Anna: Didn't you go to the beach?

Ryan: Yes, a bit later in the day. I went swimming in the sea and then sat and chatted to some friends in the café.

Anna: Sounds good. I didn't see my friends on Saturday – we just chatted online.

UNIT 4

🔊 Track 08

Listening Part 2

Narrator: For each question, write the correct answer in the gap. Write one word or a number or a date or a time. You have ten seconds to look at Part Two.

Narrator: You will hear the secretary of a running club telling new members about the club.

Woman: Good morning, everyone. It's always great to welcome new members to the running club. I'm the club secretary and my name's Daniella Black. You'll find my email address on our website. The club gets together one evening every week, on Tuesdays. I post information about the runs on Sundays. As it's summer now, we're still meeting at seven o'clock. However, that will change next month. In the autumn and winter we meet at five thirty. We do two practice runs each week: one is 12 kilometres, and there's a shorter run for beginners and children that's six kilometres. You can choose which run you want to do. When the weather's good, we run through the forest, but if it's wet we run on the paths through the park. We also have a special club day every year. This year that'll be on June 18th at Jack's Hill. Last year we had a barbecue at the house of a club member, and this year we're going to have a picnic. So does anyone have any questions?

Narrator: Now listen again.

Narrator: That is the end of Part Two.

UNIT 5

🔊 Track 09

Daniel: I went on my first cruise last month. I'm a journalist for a student magazine, and a cruise company invited me to go on one of their ships. The company wants more young people to try cruises.

The cruise ship I went on was enormous: it had 15 floors, like a high building, and there were over 2,800 passengers on it. It was a two-week cruise from Turkey, around Greece and ending in Italy.

I got on the ship and went straight to my room. I took everything out of my suitcase, put my suitcase under my bed and went to look around the ship. There were 10 restaurants, and during the cruise, I tried them all! The food was fantastic. You could choose from lots of different types, and there were different menus in the restaurants every day.

Before I left, I was worried about being bored on the cruise, but I soon stopped thinking that. In fact, there was too much to do! We stopped at a new place nearly every day, and there were tours at each one. It was very tiring. And on the boat there were swimming pools, a running track, a gym and exercise classes.

I was surprised about the age of people on the ship because they were not all very old! Most of the people on the cruise were between the ages of 40 and 60, but there are also some young families and a few people the same age as me. It was really easy to make friends, too, because you sat with the same group of people each night for dinner, and you soon got to know everyone very well. I will certainly go on a cruise again!

UNIT 6

🎵 Track 10

Listening Part 5

Narrator: For each question, choose the correct answer. You have fifteen seconds to look at Part Five.

Narrator: You will hear Pippa talking to her friend Mario about desserts in a restaurant. Which dessert does each person want?

Mario: Right, Pippa, we have to order desserts over there, at that food bar. I'll go and order for everyone.

Pippa: Great, thanks, Mario.

Mario: So what does everyone want, Pippa? I'll write it down.

Pippa: Well I'd like the fresh mango – my favourite fruit.

Mario: OK, and David, will he have fruit too? He usually does.

Pippa: Yes, but not the pears. He wants the strawberries – with cream, not ice cream.

Mario: OK. I love strawberries too but coconut rice is on the menu – the best dessert in the world! I'll have that.

Pippa: OK, Mario. Now, Helen couldn't decide between the chocolate cake and the ice cream but chose the cake in the end.

Mario: Right. And Sarah?

Pippa: She'd like the baked pears – she usually has coconut rice here but she wants to try something new.

Mario: OK. What about Paul? He doesn't like desserts much, does he?

Pippa: Not usually, but he'd like the yoghurt and honey. You can have biscuits with it, but he doesn't want any.

Mario: Great. That's everyone. I'll go and order.

Narrator: Now listen again.

Narrator: That is the end of Part Five.

UNIT 7

🎵 Track 11

Johannes: I can't believe how many clubs this university has, Carla!

Carla: I know – there are 286 on this list! It's impossible to choose!

Johannes: But I think it's really important to do club activities as well as studying. If you study all the time, you just get bored and you don't learn as much.

Carla: I totally agree, Johannes. But how can we choose from so many?

Johannes: OK, so do you want to do some exercise? Or do some art? Or social clubs, where you can just have fun hanging out with people? There are clubs for the course subjects, too, like the history club or IT club.

Carla: I'm not interested in those – we spend enough time studying them! I'd like to do some exercise so I can keep healthy … but not running or tennis … something different …

Johannes: Right, well these look exciting … snow sports, or flying club …

Carla: Oh look – what's this one: the 'parkour' club?

Johannes: Oh yes … I've done that. But I hated it – it was really hard. It's a bit like what you do in a gym, but without any equipment, and you do it outside – you run and jump over walls and stairs in the street, things like that.

Carla: Really? That sounds good. I think I'll try that. What about you, Johannes? Do you want to do exercise or art, or something else?

Johannes: Well, I want to do some volunteering – you know, work for no money, helping people. A group of students from our university goes and helps at the hospital. They visit sick children and take them presents, or play board games with them, or just hang out with them.

Carla: That's a great idea, Johannes. And you want to be a doctor, so it will help you with your job in the future.

Johannes: That's right.

UNIT 8

🎵 Track 12

Listening Part 4

Narrator: For each question, choose the correct answer. One. You will hear a woman talking about her home. What sort of home is it?

Woman: It's not very big but it's on two floors and it's got three bedrooms. It's a traditional type of building in this area, and is about 100 years old. The best thing is the views from all the windows: you can see fields and the river, and mountains in the distance. We're a long way from the nearest city or town.

Narrator: Now listen again.

Narrator: Two. You will hear a man talking to his wife about a sofa. What are they discussing?

Man: It'll be great to have a new sofa.

Woman: Yes, I can't wait for it to come. It'll look great under the window.

Man: Actually I think it'll be too high for there. It'll be better on the wall opposite.

Woman: But the bookshelf's there. I don't want to move that.

Man: Let's wait until it's here. Then we can decide.

Narrator: Now listen again.

Narrator: Three. You will hear a woman talking to her friend about her flat.

Why doesn't she want to live in it any more?

Woman: I've decided to look for another flat.

Man: Really? Because of your new job?

Woman: Well it will take me longer to get to work now. But that's not it. The problem is that my cousin is going to come and live with me and we'll need another bedroom.

Man: That's nice – and it will be cheaper for two of you to live together.

Woman: I hope so.

Narrator: Now listen again.

Narrator: Four. You will hear a man telling a friend about a problem in his apartment building.

What is there a problem with?

Woman: Did you get home OK last night?

Man: Well, I was trying to get from the garage in the basement up to my floor last night. I got in and pressed the button for the third floor and nothing happened. It was so annoying. I had to walk up the stairs with all my shopping.

Woman: Oh dear.

Narrator: Now listen again.

Narrator: Five. You will hear a woman telling her friend about her parents' new house.

What does she like best about it?

Woman: I went to my mum and dad's new place at the weekend.

Man: So what's it like?

Woman: Well, the garden's lovely but the kitchen is very small.

Man: So you don't like it much?

Woman: Oh, I do, especially the living room. It has a lovely view out over the park.

Narrator: Now listen again.

Narrator: That is the end of Part Four.

UNIT 9

🎧 Track 13

Listening Part 3

Narrator: For each question, choose the correct answer.
You have twenty seconds to look at Part Three.

Narrator: You will hear Laura talking to her friend Otto about Marla, the place where they live.

Narrator: Now listen to the conversation.

Laura: Otto, you've lived in Marla for a month now. What do you think of it?

Otto: Well actually, Laura, I know it's a small town, but it's the biggest place I've ever lived in! Our last house was in a little village on an island.

Laura: I've never lived in a city, have you?

Otto: No, but I'd like to – it'd be great to have all those shops and cinemas …

Laura: Yes, it would be great. I'm so bored here in Marla. And I'd really like to be able to go to the theatre.

Otto: I like it here.

Laura: What do you like about Marla?

Otto: Lots of things. For example, I know nearly everyone in my street already, and they all smile and talk to me when they see me.

Laura: That's nice.

Otto: And of course, the mountains around Marla are amazing.

Laura: Yes, they are. They're a great place to do lots of activities, like climbing – I know you love doing that.

Otto: Exactly. And there are lots of other things to do – I'm planning to get a mountain bike soon – I think that will be fun.

Laura: That's a good idea, Otto. Actually, my brother does a lot of activities. You should meet him – I think you'll get on very well with him.

Otto: I'd like that, Laura.

Narrator: Now listen again.

Narrator: That is the end of Part Three.

UNIT 10

🎧 Track 14

Listening Part 2

Narrator: For each question, write the correct answer in the gap. Write one word or a number or a date or a time. You have ten seconds to look at Part Two.

Narrator: You will hear an advertisement for a new department store.

Woman: Your new Richards Department Store will soon be open! The fantastic new store is in Victoria Square. It's right in the city centre, and very easy to get to on public transport – only a five-minute walk from the underground – and the station is beside the store.

The store will open in June. The first day is the 15th, when it'll open at 10 o'clock. From the 16th of June, it opens at nine o'clock, which will be the normal opening time. It will be open Monday to Saturday, and will close every night at half past eight. Last shoppers can enter the store at eight o'clock.

The new store has two floors of clothes above our large supermarket on the ground floor. Above the clothes you'll find furniture, and then our amazing restaurant and café. That's up on the fourth floor.

If you come in the first week we open, we will give away a free pen to every customer and all the bags will be half price. So come and shop!

Narrator: Now listen again.

Narrator: That is the end of Part Two.

UNIT 11

 Track 15

Listening Part 1

Narrator: For each question, choose the correct answer.

Now we are ready to start. Look at question one.

Where is Anna going next week?

Man: Are you doing anything next week for the holidays?

Woman: Yes, I'm going to see my grandpa.

Man: Oh – the one who lives in the mountains, or the one who lives by the sea?

Woman: The one from the mountains, but I'm not staying with him there. We're going to meet in the city because we both want to see some exhibitions.

Narrator: Now listen again.

Narrator: Two. What is Alejandro going to buy?

Woman: Have you decided what you want to buy yet, Alejandro?

Man: Yes – I'm not going to get the jacket. I haven't got enough money.

Woman: The jeans are quite expensive, too …

Man: But there's a big discount on them, so I'll get them, but not the belt. I don't need that.

Woman: OK.

Narrator: Now listen again.

Narrator: Three. In which month does Antonio's English course start?

Woman: So when does your English course start, Antonio?

Man: Next month. I chose the June course because I wanted to do my other exams before it, and they're all in the last two weeks of May. The course is every weekday for the whole month.

Woman: So will you have a holiday after that, in July?

Man: Yes, if I have the money!

Narrator: Now listen again.

Narrator: Four. What time does the shop close?

Man: What's the matter, Gina?

Woman: I've started making a cake but there aren't any eggs!

Man: Oh dear – I had them for lunch! I'll run to the shop down the road – it stays open until half past six, doesn't it?

Woman: Actually it shuts at six o'clock, and it's quarter past now.

Man: Sorry!

Narrator: Now listen again.

Narrator: Five. What kind of music will there be at tonight's concert?

Man: I'm going to a concert tonight.

Woman: Oh? Is it to see that famous musician who plays the violin?

Man: No, it's someone new who plays the trumpet.

Woman: Oh right. I'm surprised you're going – I thought you only liked guitar music.

Man: The guitar's great, but I love seeing people play other instruments really well too.

Narrator: Now listen again.

Narrator: That is the end of Part One.

UNIT 12

 Track 16

Listening Part 4

Narrator: For each question, choose the correct answer.

One. You will hear a woman asking her friend James about college.

What did James do this morning?

Woman: What were you doing at college this morning, James?

Man: I was finding out about schools in our city for a history project. I found some great photos and newspaper articles, as well as a useful book, so I wrote lots of notes! It's important for me to get a good mark for this essay, so I don't fail the history course.

Narrator: Now, listen again.

Narrator: Two. You will hear a woman talking about school. What was her favourite subject at school?

Woman: Mr Richards taught my favourite subject at school. He was a great teacher because he wanted everyone in the class to take part in our performances, even the students that didn't want to act. He asked them to sing a song, for example, or to paint the walls around the stage. He always made his lessons a lot of fun.

Narrator: Now listen again.

Narrator: Three. You will hear a man talking to a friend about an exam. Why did their friend Tom fail the exam?

Man: Tom didn't pass the biology exam.

Woman: Tom didn't? That's unusual for him. Was he ill?

Man: He was fine, but he said he wrote too much, and then he didn't have time to answer all the questions.

Woman: What a shame. You both did so much work to prepare for that exam.

Man: Oh well, he can take it again in September.

Narrator: Now listen again.

Narrator: Four. You will hear a girl talking to her dad about university. What does the girl's dad suggest that she does?

Woman: My maths teacher wants me to do a maths degree.

Man: Is that what you want to do?

Woman: Yes. I was thinking about doing physics but I enjoy maths more, so I've decided to do that.

Man: Great. Why don't you look at different universities and see which offer the best courses for you?

Woman: I'll do that today.

Narrator: Now listen again.

Narrator: Five. You will hear a woman talking to a friend about her job. Why does she like her job?

Man: Are you still enjoying your job at the farm?

Woman: Yes – I'd like to earn a bit more one day, but the work's brilliant. I know much more about farming now than when I started – college certainly doesn't teach you everything you need to know! I don't see the manager much, but the other staff are lovely.

Man: Great!

Narrator: Now listen again.

Narrator: That is the end of Part Four.

UNIT 13

🔊 **Track 17**

Listening Part 3

Narrator: For each question, choose the correct answer. You have twenty seconds to look at Part Three.

Narrator: You will hear Jo talking to her mum about her mum's Grandpa Bill.

Now listen to the conversation.

Jo: Mum, look at this old book!

Mum: Where did you find that?

Jo: Well, I was looking for my blue jewellery box in the cupboard in the living room. I found this instead. I'm not sure why it wasn't on the bookshelf.

Mum: That book belonged to my Grandpa Bill.

Jo: I never knew him. What was he like?

Mum: Lovely. He didn't talk much, but he smiled all the time. But he didn't like big groups of people, so never came to family parties.

Jo: Is he the grandpa with the horse?

Mum: Yes, but it was old so I didn't ride it. Grandpa read lots of books, and he baked bread. I loved making different kinds with him.

Jo: And what about his job? Wasn't he a factory worker?

Mum: For many years he was. He liked it, but he wanted me to be a doctor, and wasn't happy when I became a teacher!

Jo: So where did he meet his wife, your Grandma Annie?

Mum: She worked in a theatre, selling tickets …

Jo: And he met here there?

Mum: That's right. He invited her to the cinema, and soon after that they got married in the town hall.

Narrator: Now listen again.

Narrator: That is the end of Part Three.

UNIT 14

🔊 **Track 18**

Listening Part 5

Narrator: For each question, choose the correct answer. You have fifteen seconds to look at Part Five.

Narrator: You will hear Steve talking to a friend about his family and sports. What sport does each person do?

Woman: This is a great picture of you with your team, Steve!

Man: Thanks!

Woman: Have you played cricket all your life?

Man: Yes, since I was seven.

Woman: Does your sister play too?

Man: She thinks cricket's really boring. Her sport's volleyball and she's very good at it – better than she was at basketball. She doesn't play that now. She's got a match tomorrow, actually.

Woman: Are all your family going to her match?

Man: My brother can't because he's got a competition.

Woman: He runs, doesn't he?

Man: Yes. He's got races this morning and the long jump this afternoon.

Woman: What a sporty family!

Man: Yes! It's probably because of my granddad. He was a rugby player.

Woman: Oh yes. Does he still play?

Man: No, but he loves tennis and badminton.

Woman: Really? And what about your parents?

Man: Mum spends a lot of her free time at the pool.

Woman: Right. Is your dad sporty?

Man: Not very. He played basketball with us when we were younger, and he's always liked kicking a ball around in the park with friends. He still plays football sometimes.

Woman: That's nice.

Narrator: Now listen again.

Narrator: That is the end of Part Five.

ACKNOWLEDGEMENTS

The authors and publishers acknowledge the following sources of copyright material and are grateful for the permissions granted. While every effort has been made, it has not always been possible to identify the sources of all the material used, or to trace all copyright holders. If any omissions are brought to our notice, we will be happy to include the appropriate acknowledgements on reprinting and in the next update to the digital edition, as applicable.

Key: ST = Starter, U = Unit

Photography
The following images are sourced from Getty Images.

ST: Zero Creatives/Cultura; sturti/E+; Darren Walsh/Chelsea FC; **U1:** Andrew Wakeford/Photodisc; Tim Robberts/The Image Bank; Caiaimage/Agnieszka Olek; Hispanolistic/E+; PeopleImages/E+; **U2:** Scott Brawn/EyeEm; Jungang Yan/Moment; Westend61; Jesse Kraft/ EyeEm; Ogphoto/E+; Shaun Egan/DigitalVision; 35007/E+; Ove Eriksson/Nordic Photos; WWW.Paulgracephotography.co.uk/moment; B. Anthony Stewart/National Geographic Image Collection; **U3:** Frans Sellies/Moment; Maskot; Hero Images; MGTS/E+; **U4:** Dougal Waters/ DigitalVision; SolStock/E+; Ujang Wahyudin/EyeEm; **U5:** Jamie Grill/The Image Bank; Don Hammond; Dong Wenjie/Moment; **U6:** Dorling Kindersley; James Baigrie/The Image Bank; Creative Crop/ DigitalVision; David Marsden/Photolibrary; Edelweiss Spykerman/ EyeEm; Ian Dikhtiar/EyeEm; letty17/E+; Piotr Marcinski/EyeEm; lucia meler/Moment; Hero Images; Bojan89/iStock/Getty Images Plus; **U7:** Dave J Hogan/Getty Images Entertainment; Hero Images; Tempura/E+; Noel Hendrickson/DigitalVision; **U8:** ultraforma/iStock/Getty Images Plus; Jeff Overs/BBC News & Current Affairs; Francesco Riccardo Iacomino/AWL Images; Alexander Spatari/Moment; **U9:** Caiaimage/ Tom Merton/OJO+; PeopleImages/E+; Hero Images; Cultura Exclusive/ Kevin Kozicki; Flashpop/DigitalVision; **U10:** Pete Ark/Moment; Martin Konopka/EyeEm; Colors Hunter/Moment; JohnGollop/iStock/ Getty Images Plus; Kerstin Rüttgerodt/Moment; Flottmynd/Moment; junyyeung/iStock/Getty Images Plus; TonyV3112/iStock Editorial/Getty Images Plus; **U11:** Westend61; Halfpoint Images/Moment; d3sign/ Moment; **U12:** vgajic/E+; Hinterhaus Productions/DigitalVision; Maskot; **U13:** benimage/iStock/Getty Images Plus; D_Zheleva/iStock/ Getty Images Plus; AndyL/E+; Bco88/iStock/Getty Images Plus; vav63/ iStock/Getty Images Plus; Indeed; pic_studio/iStock/Getty Images Plus; Jamie Grill; Letizia Le Fur/ONOKY; AleksandarGeorgiev/E+; fotoVoyager/E+; **U14:** John Coletti/The Image Bank; Jiraporn Gurle/ EyeEm; bjeayes/iStock/Getty Images Plus; Gannet77/E+; petrenkod/ iStock/Getty Images Plus; Federico Scotto/Moment; Sam Edwards/OJO Images; Nigel Owen/Action Plus; Jun Tsukuda/Aflo.

The following images are sourced from other sources/libraries.

ST: M.Sobreira/Alamy Stock Photo; **U5:** Design Pics Inc./Alamy Stock Photo.

Front cover photography by Supawat Punnanon/EyeEm; Patrick Foto; fStop Images-Caspar Benson; Alexander Spatari; primeimages.

Illustrations
Chris Chalik

Audio
Produced by Ian Harker and recorded at The SoundHouse Studios, London

Page make up
EMC Design Ltd